WOMEN IN LOCAL GOVERNMENT

WOMEN IN LOCAL GOVERNMENT

A Study of Maharashtra

HAZEL D'LIMA

CONCEPT PUBLISHING COMPANY
NEW DELHI

The publication of the manuscript was financially supported by the College of Social Work, Nirmala Niketan.

First Published 1983

Published by
Naurang Rai
Concept Publishing Company
H-13 Bali Nagar
NEW DELHI-110015 (India)

Printed by
Jai Kamal Printers
at Anil Printers, Naveen Shahdara
DELHI-110032

To

Eustace
my dear brother
God's priest forever
with love

Foreword

There are not many studies of women occupying leadership positions in rural areas. This field study by Dr. Hazel D'Lima is based on interviews with 143 women members of the Panchayat Samitis and Zilla Parishads distributed in all the four divisions of Maharashtra. The women were interviewed mostly in their homes and a few in the offices of the Samitis or Parishads. The number of women interviewed works out to about 50 per cent of the actual number of women who had been elected/nominated as members of local government bodies at the time of study.

The objectives of the study were four : to find out the different social and political groups from which the women representatives were drawn, to study their outlook and the extent of their awareness of their special role as women representatives, to examine the scope and the actual degree of participation of these members in the local government bodies and in the rural community, and to identify the factors that might facilitate or impede the effective participation of women representatives.

The study of socio-economic background showed that women from the Maratha (Kshatriya and Kunbi) caste, from large land-owning families (20 acres+) and women with some education are represented to a greater degree among the sample of women interviewed than their actual proportions in the rural population. The women also tended to be drawn from families where the husband or the father was involved in political activity at the rural or the Zilla levels. Caste background, economic status and education are of course interrelated variables, but in some cases education seemed to have compensated for the lack of either appropriate caste or economic status.

A study of the personal background of these women representatives showed that their mean age was 45; they were either married or widowed; there was only one woman representative who had not been married; they had on an average about 3 children born to them though 15 per cent of the respondents were without children.

The women representatives were of the view that women should participate in social activities outside the home and some were even in favour of their taking up a job if that was possible : yet they did not want women to neglect their homes or their family life. The representatives thought a widow should remarry only if she was without any children : if she had children she should devote herself to their upbringing and not jeopardise their happiness by another marriage.

While the women representatives seemed to be generally aware of the more commonly discussed social issues and had their own views on them, they had little specific knowledge of facts—even in regard to services like balwadis, health-centres, employment projects etc. in their areas.

About 21 per cent of the women representatives were rated as active or 'high' participants in the discussions and activities of the bodies of which they were members. Another 22 per cent were 'low' participants. The rest belonged to the 'medium' category.

Beginning with these simple distributions the author goes on to show the relationship between social background variables and the degree of participation of the women representatives in the samiti and parishad bodies. She found that a woman's participation was significantly related to education—her own as well as her husband's and father's education. Even if the woman came from an economically well off group her participation would not be active unless she was herself educated.

Following from this the author goes on to argue for special training being provided to women representatives in local bodies. They have had no such opportunity. In many cases they have been 'co-opted' as members of the Samiti or the Parishad : so that the political education that takes place when a candidate has to *win* an election is also often absent in their case.

As the author points out statutory representation for women is not an end in itself. It is expected to be a step in promoting women's participation in national life.

On the basis of the data from the study the author says that women of upper castes, wives of big landowners and politically influential persons tend to predominate in the positions reserved for women in local bodies. She asks, "How can women who enter the structrue of Panchayati Raj because of their protected ascriptive status, really contribute towards the development of rural society, specially the weaker sections ?"

Though based on a small sample this is altogether a penetrating study of women's participation in local bodies. It has involved difficult field work in remote rural areas. The author is, therefore, able to add meaningful details and insights to what otherwise could have been a merely statistical descriptive exercise. She has raised pertinent questions and made useful suggestions for enabling women representatives to gain a better awareness of their social situation and the role they can play, in their capacity as members of decision-making bodies in rural areas.

M. S. GORE

Vice-Chancellor
University of Bombay,
Bombay

Preface

As a social worker interested in the contribution that women can make in the important task of nation-building, the subject of women's development has been of great interest to the researcher. The more women grow in awareness of their own potential as well as of existing social need, the better the response they will be able to make in the field of national development.

The awakening of women in India towards a society where justice and brotherhood prevail, can best be achieved by a woman to woman contact. Even though men have played a pioneering role in the cause of women in India, their role has been effective in bringing about constitutional and legal changes in the status of women. For these changes to affect the life-pattern of the vast majority of women in this country, women leaders must be found who can penetrate into streets and villages, homes and hearths in order to create awareness and motivation for action. The cultural pattern of Indian society is such that social progress among women can be promoted effectively through the media of personal relationships among them. It is women who can inspire confidence and the stimulus for social change especially among their sisters in rural areas. Hence, effective leadership among women must come from the ranks of women themselves.

The interest of the researcher has been increasingly directed to the development of women in rural areas because the rural population forms 80 per cent of the country's total population. To ignore their existence as it happens when one succumbs to the attractions of urbanisation, is to work for an illusory development which will never satisfy the legitimate aspirations of the masses. Such uneven development only aggravates the problem of social injustice. When the overwhelming majority of women in India today are to make their contribution towards women's development from their villages, it is necessary that professional social work which has addressed itself mostly to urban problems be interested in the development of this sector so that rural women may be second to none in playing the role expected of them.

The presence of women in the panchayati raj structure is an indication of the collaboration that is desired of them in the rural development of the country. Women's presence on panchayat bodies opens a way for them to make their voice heard and thus bring to the fore the rich content of feminine thought and action in the development of a people. It is now twenty years since the Government of Maharashtra introduced the statutory representation of women on panchayat bodies. There is need to investigate the impact of this statutory presence of women in panchayati raj. It is necessary to know whether the new social position of women on local self-governing bodies such as the panchayat structures in rural areas is a mere formality that is being observed or whether it is an instrument of dynamic development among women.

In order to see the present position and role of women in panchayat bodies it is essential to understand the social development that has taken place among the women of this country through the history of modern India. Woman, in the panchayat structure today, has her roots in the rural past. Her present position symbolises both an achievement and an aspiration. The achievement is the acceptance of woman in positions of public responsibility, an acceptance which acquires greater significance in the traditionalism of the rural context. The aspiration is the hope embodied, to draw forth in full, the feminine contribution to national development.

HAZEL D'LIMA

Principal
College of Social Work
Nirmala Niketan, Bombay
29 November 1982

Acknowledgements

It is with great joy that I express my gratitude to all who have helped in the completion of this study for it was a challenge for me specially to take the plunge into rural Maharashtra in an effort to locate the women in the sample distributed all over the districts.

I am most grateful to Dr. M.S. Gore who as Director of the Tata Institute of Social Sciences gave me his expert guidance and enabled me to complete my doctoral thesis. His encouragement led me towards the publication of this book. Despite his present numerous tasks as Vice Chancellor, he has graciously consented to write the Foreword to this study.

I would also like to thank the staff of the Tata Institute of Social Sciences for their assistance rendered in so many ways, from consultation and discussion, to providing facilities for library-work and data-processing.

The government administrative staff at the Zilla Parishad and Panchayat Samiti offices were most accommodating with regard to my schedule of visits and were it not for their consideration in the matter of transport and boarding, I would not have been able to complete the task of data-collection. I also recall with gratitude the hospitality received during my travels in the districts, from gram sevikas, mukhya-sevikas and several convents of sisters who went out of their way to make for my comfort.

To the women, members of the Zilla Parishads and Panchayat Samitis whom I interviewed, I owe a special debt of gratitude for it has been an unforgettable experience to be welcomed in their village homesteads and share so closely the simplicity and spontaneity of the rural atmosphere.

My colleagues at Nirmala Niketan, specially Miss Dorothy Baker, were a source of constant support and encouragement, facilitating the use of the library and helping in various ways especially to get the manuscripts ready. I am deeply indebted to them for their abiding interest and concern.

Finally, I thank all who have helped me, innumerable friends along the way, whose goodwill and counsel have contributed towards the making of this publication.

Contents

Glossary

Panchayati Raj (*PR*)	:	A three-tier system of local self-government in rural areas, where the lower tiers at the village and block levels are controlled by the upper tier at the district level.
Gram Panchayat (*GP*)	:	Local government body of the PR system at the village level.
Panchayat Samiti (*PS*)	:	Local government body of the PR system at the block level (a block comprises 60-100 villages).
Zilla Parishad (*ZP*)	:	Local government body of the PR system at the district level holding control over the two lower bodies.
Taluka	:	a sub-division of a district.
Maratha	:	a dominant agricultural caste of Maharashtra. Among the sub-castes are the Maratha Kashtriyas claiming association with the warrior group e.g. Shivaji Maratha ; Maratha Kunbi (agricultural landowners) and those belonging to the artisan and service sectors, e.g. shepherds gardeners, barbers, washermen.
Jagirdar, Izzar	:	Names denoting persons who were given possession of large portions of land.
Sabhapati	:	Chairman of the PS.
Upsabhapati	:	Vice-chairman of the PS.
Sarpanch	:	President of the GP.
Upsarpanch	:	Vice-president of the GP.
Mahila Mandal	:	A Women's Association.
Shibir	:	A Camp.
Beedi	:	A locally produced cigarette with tobacco rolled in a dry leaf.

Gram Sevika	:	A village-level woman worker in charge of activities for woman and children.
Mukhya Sevika	:	A block-level woman officer in charge of activities for women and children, and for co-ordinating the work of gram sevikas.
Sharada Utsav	:	A religious festival specially celebrated by women in rural areas.
Huldi Kum Kum	:	A joyous get-together of women who greet one another by applying coloured powder on each other's foreheads as a sign of welcome.
Bhajan	:	A religious song.
Griha Kalyan Kendra	:	A welfare centre to promote activities among rural women.
Balwadi	:	A nursery school.
'Ho manner bai'	:	A phrase in Marathi meaning a 'yes' woman.
Shudra	:	A person belonging to a low caste.
Swaraj	:	The Hindi word for 'self-government'.

Abbreviations

GP	—	Gram Panchayat
PS	—	Panchayat Samiti
ZP	—	Zilla Parishad
GS	—	Gram Sevika
MS	—	Mukhya Sevika
PR	—	Panchayati Raj
CEO	—	Chief Executive Officer
BDO	—	Block Development Officer
FYP	—	Five Year Plan
CD	—	Community Development
FCW	—	Family and Child Welfare
ANP	—	Applied Nutrition Programme
EGS	—	Employment Guarantee Scheme

List of Tables

1

THE SOCIAL EMERGENCE OF WOMEN IN MODERN INDIA

THE realisation that women can play a more significant role than generally permitted by society has seen a new awakening over the past decades of modern history. All over the world there has been a multiplication of seminars, conferences, studies, research, documentation on women's status and role in all walks of life. It is interesting to note how political and social events have served to focus attention on the place of women in society and have served as a springboard of action in their favour. In India, the effort to restore to woman her rights as a person may be traced across the social and political events that affected the destiny of the country from the 18th century onwards. Thus one may follow the stages of development in the status of women through the pre-independence and post-independence periods.

THE PRE-INDEPENDENCE PERIOD

This period may be taken as extending from the latter half of the 18th century to the middle of the 20th century. During this time, the most important movements in the life of the country as also in the social development of women, were :

(1) the Social Reform Movement, and
(2) the Nationalist Movement.

Underlying both these movements was the aspiration for liberation : liberation of the human person, liberation of the nation. This quest for freedom drew inspiration from the ideological renaissance blowing in from the West, its emphasis being humanism which placed man as "centre and sanction" of the universe (Cheyney ; 1959 : 541). The seeds of revolutionary thought had already wrought radical changes in the socio-political structures of France and America ; the philosophy of liberalism gradually led 18th century Europe to move away from monarchy to more democratic forms of government. The spread of this ideology began to raise questions in India as to the legitimacy of colonial rule and the desirability of self-government. The deplorable effects of the Industrial Revolution in the victimisation of men, women and children awakened a sense of revolt against social injustice. A wave of humanitarianism rose up, expressing itself in a series of reforms to defend the unprotected, the deprived and oppressed members of society.

This mighty surge of humanism, liberalism and humanitarianism which was affecting the countries of the world at large, could not leave India untouched. Its impact was facilitated by the onset of British Rule which also increased the contacts of educated Indians abroad. As a result, two phases of social change ensued : social reform and political independence each of which will be reviewed in the light of their impact on the social development of women.

The social reform movement

The Social Reform Movement focussed special attention on the social status of two sectors of the population : women and the backward castes. Of the two, the cause of women's rights received greater attention in the name of social justice. Ram Mohan Roy, "Father of Modern India" as he is known, boldly attacked the inhuman practices imposed upon women in the shape of sati and the unhappy treatment meted out to widows. The courageous stand of Keshab Chunder Sen and several other enlightened thinkers helped withstand the powerful onslaught of 'orthodox' opposition to the cause. Their agitation won increasing support leading to the promulgation of a series of laws against the prevalent injustice towards women, particularly the practice of sati. The social reforms in Bengal as a movement for women's social emancipation gradually spread to other parts of the country.

Maharashtra was not long in taking the lead and a series of illustrious men, chiefly from the western region of the State, boldly stood for the cause of women's emancipation. Since the present study is located in the State of Maharashtra, it is of interest to trace the features of the social reform movement and its impact on women, in this particular State.

A brief recapitulation of the socio-political history of Maharashtra just before the British Raj, finds it the home of the powerful Maratha kingdom founded by Shivaji and later ruled by the Peshwas who were the Prime Ministers of the Peshwa kings. The Peshwa rulers were Brahmins who enjoyed a high status in Maratha society by virtue of their ritual status and their learning. Proximity to the ruling class generally brought in economic benefits and literacy enabled them to enjoy a position of superiority over other sectors of the population. However women from the upper castes whose social status had followed a downward trend during the medieval period continued to remain in the background of social life limited within the four walls of their homes and remaining more or less under the continual protection of male members in the family. The unfolding of their life-span left little room for personal decisions, especially regarding their movement and behaviour outside the home. The status of women was thus patterned in somewhat varied shades among all castes and classes. However, in the early stages of the social reform movement, the spotlight was focussed mainly on women from the high castes. At the time, caste and economic status were almost synonymous. The process of sanskritization by which the lower caste groups tended to imitate the traditionalism of the upper castes also reinforced the conservative attitude towards women.

With the advent of the British in India, institutionalised education became more widespread and the class of people who benefited most from these services were the Brahmins. Educated Brahmins also inculcated the new liberal values which made them sensitive to some of the social practices constraining their own mothers and sisters and they reacted strongly to the injustice of the situation. They publicly attacked existing attitudes and practices which were discriminatory towards women. They braved the opposition which raised the bogey of religion to thwart their effort at social change.

Outstanding among the early social reformers of Maharashtra, who championed the cause of women are Vishnushastri Pandit, Jotirao Phule, Mahadev Govind Ranade and Dhondo Keshav Karve. Encouraged by the support of friends and undaunted by the waves of opposition, these men zealously upheld the cause of women's education and the remarriage of widows. In their own homes they first adopted what they preached as advocates of women's freedom. Exemplary reformers, some of them married widows in the face of social ostracism. They laboured in the task of teaching their own wives and encouraging their development as to bring them into the forefront among the women of their times. Savitriba i Phule, Ramabai Ranade and Anandibai Karve would never have had education nor built up courage and conviction to publicly support the social rights of women had it not been for the staunch support of their husbands. The education of these women in no way disturbed the harmony of conjugal life as was understood then by the orthodox view. The reformers blazed a new path of social progress—not by mere self-achievement but in partnership with women.

As Bengal can claim the honour of having one of her sons, Ram Mohan Roy, known as 'Father of Modern India, so can Maharashtra claim as her daughter, Pandita Ramabai Saraswati, who has earned the title of "Mother of Modern India" (Sengupta ; 1970 : 38). She can indeed be held up as the 'Symbol of Modern Indian Womanhood'. Educated in Sanskrit at a time when women were barred from learning the Hindu scriptures ; choosing to marry only at the age of 21, when child-marriage was customary, and that too, a Chitpavan Brahmin taking as her husband one whom Hindu orthodoxy labelled "shudra" : her widespread tours, lecturing to national and international audiences, all give to the Pandita, an aura of feminine greatness, unique in the annals of Indian womanhood. Pandita Ramabai, as also Anandibai Joshi present a most inspiring portrait of the emancipated woman : devoted to their families, ready to spare no effort to overcome cultural inhibitions and prejudice in the pursuit of knowledge and human understanding, orienting their life's ambition to the service of their less fortunate sisters.

Two extracts from newspapers of that period give an insight into the social position of women almost a hundred years ago : A Marathi paper, *Subodh Patrika*, thus reports a social function which Pandita Ramabai attended : "Pandita Ramabai arrived in Ahmednagar on Saturday, 7th October, 1882 for a prize distribution at the Girls' school. Many Europeans and Indians were present. This was the first event in town when 'native' women attended a public function, which is a sure sign of future female reforms—a very auspicious thing indeed !" (Sengupta ; 1970 : 19). In 1889 when Pandita Ramabai's Sharada Sadan (a home for widows) was started in Bombay near Chowpatty, the *Indu Parkash*, reporting the inauguration at which Mrs. Kashibai Kanetkar was asked to preside, says : "This was the first instance of an Indian woman presiding over a function like this". (Sengupta ; 1970 : 183). Pandita Ramabai's illustrious contemporary D. K. Karve speaking at the centenary celebrations held in her honour said :

> I got my inspiration from that institution (Ramabai' Sharada Sadan) for starting the widows' home in 1896...Pandita Ramabai must be classed as one of the great builders of Modern India.

It was mainly Jotirao Phule and Pandita Ramabai who drew attention to the fact that social discrimination was practiced specially against woman and the shudra. The status of women was in a way likened to that of the shudra—both having no access to educational institutions, both under servile dependence : the women to her husband or senior male members and the shudra to the higher castes. Jotirao Phule made an effort to reach out to women of all castes in the process of social emancipation but there were difficulties, as initially social reform had to be channellised through the elite class. The British educational system being more of a literary pursuit, it appealed to the higher castes and those who aspired to enter the bureaucracy in power, or the learned professions. It followed that women belonging to these classes were better placed to benefit from the educational facilities available. A note in the Bombay Guardian (1850) expresses the limitations of the existing educational system : "It is one of the great defects of all our educational institutions in India, that no provision is made for popular education. We educate the rich who are able to educate themselves and make no provision for the elevation of the Kunbee and Pariah" (Keer ; 1974 : 47). In these circumstances, the social emergence of women belonging to the backward classes remained almost neglected. It was hoped that the facilities available to the higher class would gradually percolate down to reach the lower classes, but such percolation takes its time. Even today it is observed that education remains the privilege of higher caste and economically dominant groups. Despite such limitations it is to be recognised that the spirit of the social reform movement did find effective expression in a series of legislative measures which marked the beginning of national policy in favour of women.

Social reform and legislation concerning women

The cumulative result of the efforts of social reformers combined with the support of ruling authority, led to the promulgation of a series of laws preventing the malpractices that had crept into the social system due to a poor concept of woman's position in society. The legislation condemning infanticide in 1804 benefited women more specially as the practice of female infanticide was found to be fairly common in a culture that made woman totally dependent on the family for life.

The Bengal Sati Regulation Act of 1829 was later made applicable to the whole country and paved the way for the Widow Remarriage Act of 1856. Again, the Married Women's Property Act in 1874 gave woman the right to her own property and earnings (Baig ; 1974 : 215). In 1891, society was able to raise the age of consent for marriage from 10 to 12 years. The above legislation may seem like making very small concessions which hardly measure up to the status of woman as enshrined in the Constitution, yet in the social context of the times, they mark a notable achievement. One has only to think of the time when Karve and his wife were treated with the humiliation that was inflicted on social outcastes, or the bitter criticism of certain leaders, influential enough at the time, to oppose the passage of the Age of Consent Bill, to appreciate better the stages of gradual achievement on the way to women's social emancipation.

These early efforts relentlessly pursued, with their consequent measure of success soon gathered their own momentum. The consciousness of women's social rights opened the way for the acquisition of political rights as called for during the struggle for independence.

The nationalist movement

The early twentieth century began to resound with the cries of "Swaraj" calling all Indians to join hand in the struggle for national independence.

Whereas in 1900, legislation had barely grappled with problems such as sati, widow-marriage, prevention of child-marriage, by 1940 India stood third among the nations of the world for the political influence and position secured by her women (Cousins ; 1940 : 60). There is no doubt that the national movement towards independence has been the most potent cause of women's emergence in the socio-political life of the nation. "An important factor in social change is the emergence of a common purpose." (Ginsberg ; 1970 : 55). In the common striving of Indians towards the goal of political freedom, the voice of orthodox dissenters was at least temporarily silenced and the tide of patriotism could not be stemmed by barriers of religion, culture, or sex. "All over the world we find that revolutions, patriotic movements and political cataclysms have been favourable to women" (Menon ; 1957 : 64). In periods of national struggle, collaboration between men and women is no option, it becomes a matter of survival. Reformers of the sensitivity of Gandhi were able to welcome women's participation both as an opportunity for her own growth as a person and as a force for the independence movement.

The early leadership in women's organisations drew greatly from the inspiration of Annie Besant and Margaret Cousins who contributed much to the task of awakening the social and political consciousness of Indian women. To quote Margaret Cousins (1941 : 32) on her involvement with the women's movement :

> ......When week after week my husband and I read in daily papers of a never-ending stream of men going in deputation to the Viceroy and the Right Honourable E.S. Montagu, and never a mention of the voice of an Indian woman, all my training in organising, in taking hold of psychological movements could not be curbed, and I approached about twenty of India's best known women in public life, most of whom I had met through the Senate Meetings of Professor Karve's Indian Women's University.

In the ferment of 19th century reform there was a burgeoning of women's organisations all over the country. The first phase began around 1884 when small women's organisations began their pioneer work among illiterate women in Bengal, Maharashtra and Gujarat (Baig; 1976 : 25). Their activities were directed towards the education of women, setting up of cottage industries for poor women, offering training in teaching and nursing. The first All India Women's organisation was the Women's Indian Association which was founded in Madras in May 1917. The issue of women's franchise began to receive increasing attention during this period and since this was one of the most publicised issues of the organisation, the likelihood is strong that it was a key factor in the growth of this women's association. The interest of the organisation also widened to educational and social reform issues (Everett ; 1979 : 70, 72). The Bombay Presidency Women's Council, founded in 1918, co-ordinated the activities of women's associations in the Bombay Presidency and later joined the National Council of Women (NCWI) in India. This was an organisation of socially prominent women. Women's organisations in Bombay had started during the period of the First World War and were engaged in war work. Later the NCWI expanded the scope of its work to include social service activity. The need for women to engage in the spread of women's education led to the formation of the All India Women's Conference in October 1926. The primary interest of the Conference was to influence government policy on women in the fields of education, social service, personal law, suffrage, employment and health. Two of the Conference's most important campaigns were suffrage and Hindu Law Reform (Everett; 1979 : 75). The Conference was successful in creating a sisterhood of Hindu, Muslim, Sikh, Christian and Parsi women. Under the leadership of Sarojini Naidu, one of India's greatest heroines during the march towards Independence, the All India Women's Conference expressed to the British Government, the desire of women in favour of adult suffrage, removal of all sex disqualifications and equal opportunities for men and women to secure representation in legislative and administrative institutions. (Kaur ; 366-367).

It is of interest to quote the paragraph stating the claims of Indian women in their demand for suffrage in 1917. Some of the demands still hold good for Indian women today :

> Our interests as one-half of the people are directly affected by the demand . . . . that the members of the Council should be directed directly by the people on as broad a franchise as possible . . . . . we pray that when such a franchise is being drawn up, women may be recognised as 'people' and that it may be worded in such terms as will not disqualify our sex but allow our women the same opportunities of representation as our men. In agreeing with the demand of the above-mentioned memorandum, that a full measure of the Local Self-Government should be immediately granted, we request that it shall include the representation of our women . . . . . The precedent for including women in modern Indian political life has been a marked feature of the Indian National Congress in which since its inception, women have voted and been delegates and speakers, and which this year finds its climax in the election of a woman as its president. Thus the voice of India approves of its women being considered responsible and acknowledged citizens; and we urgently claim that, in drawing up of all provisions regarding representation, our sex shall not be made a disqualification for the exercise of the franchise or for service in public life. (Asaf Ali; 351-352).

Under Mahatma Gandhi's magnetic leadership, thousands of women from all walks of life, literate as well as illiterate, throughout the length and breadth of this vast country, gathered together in the movement for independence. Spurred by the common urge of freedom. Women dared to leave the protected walls of their homes to appear openly in public; once regarded as minors, "under the perpetual tutelage" of males, they marched side by side with men voicing their rights on public roads and courting imprisonment.

The social reform movement having preceded the freedom struggle, the social and political emancipation of woman combined to form one goal. In fact the Indian National Social Conference (founded in 1887) was closely allied with the Indian National Congress because leaders of the day wished to create a sense of political unity and social responsibility as the dual inspiration of a national spirit. Women who had come to the fore in the cause of social reform had no difficulty in orienting their social activity towards the attainment of national independence. During the pre-independence period, politics and the cause of social service went hand in hand; in fact political freedom was being claimed as the only way by which the socio-economic and cultural life of the nation could be promoted.

The two movements of social reform and national independence were born in the cradle of liberalism and developed in the fight for human rights. They were the expression of two phases of growth; development of the person, development of the nation. Unless people have opportunities for self-development they cannot participate in social development. The concern for human rights is a concern for justice and equality in society, as against the discriminatory approach that existed, specially in the case of women and backward castes. The process of social emancipation which had its initial impact on the economically well-placed high caste group with urban moorings, gradually, brought to the fore, a more cosmopolitan leadership, involving even the middle classes. The manifestation of leadership from among women in fields and factories, as a result of the political upheaval in the country had not yet come into the limelight.

THE POST-INDEPENDENCE PERIOD

The years soon after Independence gave women a constitutional status which moved her to a position of equality with men in the social, economic and political life of the nation. It is of interest to see how the constitutional status has affected the lives of the majority of Indian women across the diversity of regional backgrounds. The social status of women during this period will be viewed in the light of :

(1) Legal measures,
(2) General participation in national development, and
(3) Participation in the rural sector.

Legal measures

The Preamble to the Constitution assures to men and women the fundamental rights of liberty, equality and fraternity. Woman is guaranteed "equality before law" (Act 14) and equality of opportunity in matters relating to employment or appointment to any office under the State. [Art. 16 (1) and (2)]. The Constitution also protects woman from discrimination in these matters, on grounds of "religion, race, caste, sex, descent, place of birth, residence or any one of them." (Singh ; 1975 : p. 311). A special clause [Art. 15 (3)] empowers the State to make any special provision for women and children in spite of the existing fundamental obligation of non-discrimination among citizens (Singh ; 1975 : 298). This has enabled the State to make laws giving special protection to women in the field of labour, specially those engaged in factories, mines, plantations, shops and commercial establishments.

The Directive Principles of State Policy in Part IV of the Constitution bind States to a policy directed towards the promotion of a just social order with specific recommendations of a socio-economic nature. These principles uphold the equal right of men and women to an adequate means of livelihood; the right of equal pay for equal work for both men and women; the need to protect the health and strength of workers—men, women, children; the need to protect citizens from having to enter avocations unsuited to their age and strength merely because of economic necessity. (Art. 39). Article 42 also directs States to make provision for securing just and humane conditions of work and maternity relief.

The position of women was sought to be improved in the domain of marriage, succession, maintenance and guardianship by the passing of the Hindu Code Bill in successive stages. The passage of this legislation was fraught with difficulty and whatever be its limitation it marks the continuity of movement towards the goal of women's emancipation. Legislative measures in post-independent India, have attempted to remove age-old obstacles in the way of women's personal and social development.

The Constitution has given to woman a dignity that derives from her status as person. One may say that religious and cultural prejudice with regard to women has given way to official equality of opportunity to every woman in the country. The Constitution and the ensuing legislation are symbolic of the progress that is desired in the status of women. They have definitely opened the way for the Indian woman to emerge as a responsible person able to participate fully in all aspects of national life. However, the realisation of this goal depends on a network of socio-political factors which influence societal attitudes and the motivation for change. It is the interplay of these factors in various situations that makes for the unequal development of women despite a common constitutional norm.

General participation in national development

Soon after Independence, the country opted for a political system and a socio-economic goal in which all sectors of people would be able to make a contribution. The recognition of woman as an individual, as a member of society having a place in the political system, though a recent phenomenon, was stimulated mainly because of women's active participation in the independence movement. This recognition has earned for the Indian women a definite place in the country's planned economy "even though this realisation is still in its infancy" (Shah ; 1947 : 23). Women's contribution in post-independent India has been worthy of note chiefly through her political, educational and socio-economic involvement.

The women who had emerged as leaders during the independence struggle, continued to play an active part in the political life of the country. Several of them became members of the Constituent Assembly; an impressive number were entrusted with ministerial responsibility at Central and State levels; some held office as governors, some became members of Parliament. On international bodies women were delegated as official representatives of the country.

Political leadership among women in post-independent India was heralded by the freedom movement, chiefly among the upper and middle class educated women from urban-based areas. The growth of cities was a marked trend of the pre-independence period and they became powerful centres of social, economic and political activity. Thus, even now, the majority of women who rise to political power are those who have urban moorings and who belong to "the economic and political elite of the States" (Comm. on Status of Women; 1974 : 298).

The political struggle for independence being over, women's organisations gradually settled down to adopt programmes mainly in the field of social welfare. The National Council of Women in India

(NCWI) began to be involved in activities for women and children, chiefly in education, medical care and family planning. The All India Women's Conference which had politically-oriented leaders was represented in the Constituent Assembly and mobilised support for the Hindu Code Bill. It is an organisation that acts by stimulating public opinion on issues concerning women. Both the above organisations are urban-based. Some of the more recent organisations for women who greater concern with issues of 'social justice' and their membership is more heterogeneous. The Bhartiya Grameen Mahila Sangh (1955) has a rural focus; the National Federation of Indian Women (1954) consists of working women, a generally less affluent class, and it helps to take action against corrupt practices like hoarding, or rising prices; the Stree Shakti Jagaran (1973), a Gandhian organisation, to raise the social status of women, believes that such change can be better effected by women themselves.

One of the most important women's organisations in Maharashtra is MAVIM (Maharashtra Arthik Vikas Mahamandal) which helps the economic participation of women through co-operative endeavour. Mahila Mandals located in or close to urban surroundings are fairly active and have helped to create social awareness among women. Lately women in Maharashtra have started various publications concerning the problems, needs and role of women. In the wake of continuing discriminatory practices (e.g., dowry) and attacks on the person of women, a number of women's activist groups have swung into action.

When Margaret Cousins wished to find a band of Indian women to champion the cause of political rights, she found most of them through the Senate Meetings of Professor Karve's Indian Women's University (Cousins; 1941 : 32). This reveals the dynamic role of education in the social development of Indian women. The social reform movement which championed the cause of women's education thus prepared the way for their participation during the freedom struggle and thereby for their political role in independent India.

The new vision of national development as a "just social, political and economic order", oriented to promote the welfare of the people necessitated the breaking down of the barriers of race, religion, caste or sex so that all citizens could participate fully and equally in any area of national life. As seen earlier, during the social reform movement, such a vision ran counter to the forces of tradition which still held sway over the large masses of men and women. To build a new India meant to build a new outlook. The rigidity of the past would have to yield to the aspirations of the future. Such a social change could not be achieved without education. During the British period, the formal education of women made a beginning but the pace of educational development picked up more rapidly after independence, as shown in the following table :

TABLE 1.1 : **Progress of literacy among women in India**

Census Year	Percentage to total population
1901	0.60
1911	1.05
1921	1.81
1931	2.93
1941	7.30
1951	7.93
1961	12.95
1971	18.69
1981	24.88

Source : Government of India (Ministry of Social Welfare), Handbook of Social Welfare Statistics, 1981, p. 85.

The education of women was at first confined mostly to the primary stage but gradually there was expansion at the secondary and higher education levels. The Committee on the Status of Women (1974 : 240-241) reports that secondary and higher education (the latter even more than secondary) is largely confined to upper and middle class families in urban areas. In comparison, the education of women has made very little progress in rural areas. The percentage of literacy among women in urban areas is 47.65 as against 17.99 among women in rural areas (Government of India; 1981 : 86).

The expansion of education among urban women has led to a growth in the economic participation of this sector in service occupations and professions. There is an "increasing tendency among urban educated women to take up paid employment which reflects a gradual ideological change in social values as well as the growing economic pressure on urban middle-class families" (Comm. on Status of Women ; 1974 : 201). The increasing opportunity of employment in the tertiary sector goes hand in hand with urban expansion in the country. Today there are more women in white collar occupations such as doctors, nurses, teachers, office-workers.

"The system of education has to be adapted to the requirements of national planning." (Govt. of India; 1951 : 221). While the system of education may have benefited the requirements in the tertiary sector, leading even to a situation of overcrowding the demand for service, it has hardly benefited the large masses of women engaged in cultivation or agricultural labour. The kind of formal education that is imparted, does not prepare for a skilled performance at work and since the vast majority of female labour is employed in the primary sector, they constantly remain at the level of unskilled workers. Moreover, household and small industry have had to make room for modern large-scale industry, thus curtailing the opportunities for women's economic participation.

Thus, from the brief description above, one could summarise the emergent characteristics of women's participation in national development as follows :

1. Women have shown as increasing involvement in the political, educational and economic life of the nation.
2. The involvement is confined more to urban areas where there is greater opportunity for social participation.
3. The role of the middle-class urban woman as a paid worker outside the home has gradually come to be accepted as a norm.
4. Lack of opportunity for education, training and social contacts among women in rural areas has led to a widening gap between women in urban and rural areas, to the detriment of rural women, specially in the areas of social participation.

Participation in the rural sector

Planning in post-independent India set a high premium on rural development. The rural population, scattered over the length and breadth of the country, often in inaccessible areas, had to be reached out to and involved in the development effort. This reaching out was done through the Community Development (CD) Programme which was launched in October 1952. "Planning in a democratic State is a social process in which, in some part, every citizen should have the opportunity to participate" (Govt. of India ; 1951 : 5).

Developing nations have found that it is not enough merely to make declarations of policy or even to pass statutory enactments although these are fundamental. The most important work of government is to involve people in the administrative process and integrate communities of people in the life of the nation, enabling them to contribute fully to national progress (Ghildyal ; 1970 : p. 128). The Government has been alive to this problem ever since the dawn of independence, and the move towards increasing local self-government found expression even in the directive principles of the Constitution (Art. 40) which recommends the organisation of village panchayats. It is of interest in this study to see the position that women have found in the local communities at the rural level.

Provision for women's development was made through the activities of a new cadre of personnel specially trained and appointed for the purpose. These were the gram sevikas and mukhya sevikas appointed under the CD and Central Social Welfare Board (CSWB) Programmes which sought to promote welfare activity among women and children. In keeping with the scope of Five Year Plans, there was a gradual expansion of health and educational services which required a growing band of nurses and teachers to work in villages. These were the first examples of formal leadership among women in the rural community. Where women had not been known to engage in social activity outside the home and where such participation was frowned upon, the emergence of these new roles, born of an organised effort at development, were indeed innovatory. They blazed a path for women's public appearance in work for the rural community.

It was found, however, that community involvement which had been the leitmotif of the CD programme was not forthcoming as expected and planned for. The personnel appointed for the implementation of the programme had been mostly recruited from urban areas and their adjustment to the rural set-up was found wanting.

The need of grass-roots involvement for the implementation of the programme began to make itself felt increasingly. There was a growing realisation that development and responsibility are closely interlinked and that there can be no development worth the name if people do not feel responsible for the process. Development of the rural sector could take place only if the people were effectively drawn into the planning and implementation of schemes. The system of centralised planning and employment of personnel from outside rural areas, could not yield the expected results. It would be only a further wastage of time and money without benefit accruing to the rural community.

It was in the light of the all important goal of local participation that the Balwantrai Mehta Committee submitted its report recommending a system of democratic decentralisation. The goal of the C.D. programme had not changed but there was fresh thinking about the methods to achieve the goal. "Community development can be real only when the community understands its problems, realises its responsibilities, exercises the necessary powers through its chosen representatives......" (Govt. of India ; 1978 : 3).

In the context of the rural sector, women's development also posed the same problem : How could rural women be made more responsible for their own development ? The early gram sevikas, mukhya sevikas, health workers and teachers with their urban backgrounds were not keen on continuing service in rural areas ; the low educational backgrounds of girls in rural areas made it difficult to find qualified personnel in the rural setting ; the vastness of the rural sector made it impossible to find trained personnel to meet the outreach expected. In the face of these challenges, it became clearer that greater involvement on a voluntary basis, by local rural women was a *sine qua non* for women's development. During the period of the Third Five Year Plan, much encouragement was given to the establishment of Mahila Mandals in an effort to develop responsibility among local women. The unpreparedness of local women to take up such a responsibility as well as the apathy of the community at large in this regard have posed problems for the proper functioning of many Mahila Mandals. However, a recent study by S.P. Jain (1979) concludes that in spite of their limitations, Mahila Mandals have played an important part in helping rural women to come out of their homes and interact with the forces of social change by participation in community affairs. These social contacts have increased women's self-confidence in social functioning and have thereby helped to build up their own social status.

The recommendation of 'democratic decentralization' which led to the system of Panchayati Raj has provided yet another important channel for women's involvement in their own development as well as that of the rural community. To be on a panchayat body such as the Zilla Parishad (ZP) or Panchayat Samiti (PS) is to occupy a formal position of some power in the local community. As such, these members can play an important role in promoting the social change desired among rural women. One major objective of this study is to find out whether the channel that has been opened to women through Panchayati Raj is leading effectively towards women's development in the rural sector. In the absence of any study specifically on women involved in the structures of Panchayati Raj, the researcher felt it necessary to start by two questions : Who are the women chosen ? What are they able to do ? This exploration of the social identity and participatory pattern of women-members at the block and district levels of Panchayati Raj, was felt to be essential for an understanding of the actual and possible efficacy of their social role as members.

PANCHAYATI RAJ AND WOMEN'S DEVELOPMENT

After the launching of the Community Development Programme in 1952, the acceptance of "democratic decentralization" recommended by the Balwantrai Mehta Committee in 1957, marked the second major step forward in involving the rural population in development endeavour. The main objectives of Panchayati Raj are democratization, development and social change (Narain ; 1976 : 3). This democratic change was envisaged through a process of administrative decentralization and control by "elected bodies". The Committee made suggestions regarding the allotment of power, the exercise of responsibility and the use of resources for the effective functioning of these bodies at the levels of the village, block and the district. (Jathar ; 1964 : 55).

The abiding philosophy animating Panchayati Raj is that real development consists in the responsible participation of people.

The Panchayati Raj organisation came into existence in Maharashtra in 1962 with the establishment of Zilla Parishads and Panchayat Samitis under the Maharashtra Zilla Parishad and Panchayat Samiti Act of 1961. Though Maharashtra adopted the Panchayati Raj structure rather late, being the eleventh State to adopt the system, the pattern established was unique and it has been recognised as one of the most successful efforts in the country. What characterises the set-up in Maharashtra, is the dominant position of the Zilla Parishad to which the other bodies are linked, structurally and functionally. (Inamdar ; 1977 : 179). The three distinct features of the Panchayati Raj system in Maharashtra are :

(a) a strong organisation at the district level ;
(b) separation of the executive functions from the deliberative

and policy-making functions entrusted to the elected representatives of the people ; and

(c) direct elections to the Panchayati Raj bodies at the district level as against indirect elections from one body to another (Govt. of Maharashtra ; 1971 : 17).

The position of women in this set-up is that they are to have representation on each of the three bodies at the district, taluka and village levels. In the case of the Zilla Parishad, two women are to be "co-opted if the directly elected members do not include a woman or women". At the Panchayat Samiti level the clause is, "co-option of one woman residing in the block if such representation is not already included".

A special statute regarding women's representation on panchayat bodies may be described as the adoption of a considerate approach to women as a weaker section of society. N.R. Inamdar (1977 : 82) commenting on women's representation on these bodies, says : The need for a minimum representation of women in the Zilla Parishad was obvious". Again, speaking of the co-option of two women on the Social Welfare Committee of the Zilla Parishad (p. 185), he comments "This special representation would make it alive to the problems of these under-privileged sections." The implication is that women belong to an under-privileged section of society and are in need of being represented. The Constitution regards women and backward classes as weaker sections which are in need of special consideration.

The Committee on the Status of Women (1974 : 304) believes that the active involvement of women in the decision-making process will best be achieved by providing them with special opportunities for participation in the representative structures of local Government. The necessity for such association of women representatives is already accepted in the country and provision for reservation of seats for women through either election, co-option or nomination in these bodies has been made in their Constitutions. The Committee feels that as the statutory local self-governing institutions do not pay much attention to the subject of women's development, women's representation on Panchayat bodies should lead to a greater participation of local women in the political process and thus it would be easier to press for special programmes or schemes for women's development.

The report of the Committee on Panchayati Raj Institutions (1978 ; 140 : 141) says that by representation on panchayat bodies, the role of women in decision-making on development projects has been brought to the forefront. The Report also suggests that the decision-making role would apply specially to welfare and development programmes for women and children. The Report expects that women representatives be aware of the problems faced by women engaged in agriculture, in "the commercialisation of activities allied to agriculture" and in "mobility of labour". The growing emphasis on rural industrialisation will also necessitate women's active participation in the diversified occupational pattern for which they will need to be trained. While women occupy a comparatively small portion of the Report, it is encouraging to note that their role has been described more positively and with a greater breadth of vision. They are not merely the representatives of an under-privileged group but their involvement is regarded "as an integral part of the total development of the village community".

To summarise the role of women in Panchayat structures, one may say that women are given special representation as a weaker section of society. The goal of representation is to involve them in decision-making in the rural development effort of Panchayati Raj. Their involvement is envisaged mainly with regard to the welfare and development of women and children in rural areas. Besides the traditional activities such as Mahila Mandals and Balwadis, "their constructive decision-making and managerial roles" should be recognised and strengthened "so as to enable them to have full access to development resources and services" (Govt. of India ; 1978 : 142).

This study aims at discovering the actual performance of women representatives on Panchayat Samitis and Zilla Parishads in the light of women's socio-cultural position.

REVIEW OF LITERATURE

The Panchayati Raj programme has been launched in India since 1959 and Maharashtra implemented it in 1962. For nearly all the States, it is less than twenty years since the start of the programme in rural India. Most early evaluations focussed attention on programmes, administrative policies, staff-patterns, financial allotments.*

The study of sociological features in the programme appeared more recently, from about 1965 onwards. The members of Panchayat

* Government of Maharashtra (1971).

bodies are considered to be "formal" leaders of the rural community and are studied and referred to as the rural elite.* Since leadership is confined to men in rural areas, the panchayat structures consists mainly of men and the studies focus mainly on male leadership. Their concern is with the emerging patterns of rural leadership in the light of inevitable processes of change that affect the social pattern of functioning. Male leadership was always in the forefront and sociologists have described its salient characteristics in the traditional as well as the current social context. Women's leadership outside the home has not yet emerged in rural areas on a wide scale because traditional culture frowns on it. Whatever spark of leadership has been manifested, has not been studied in its specifically rural context. With the statute stipulating the number of women to be present on panchayat bodies, there arises a new and definite acceptance of the role of women in the socio-political life of the rural community. How does this statutory acceptance accord with actual practice in rural society? The absence of literature in this field is itself an indication of the need of a study such as the present one.

In Indian studies on women there has been a sociological slant in the early phases and reformist in the latter, specially around the post-Independence period (Mazumdar and Sharma; 1979 : 119). The early sociological studies tend to describe the status and role of women beginning from Vedic times, extolling the emancipated position of women at that time, as compared with the decadence of the long medieval period. The social reform movement and the entry of women into the struggle for independence saw publications like *Our Cause* (Nehru, 1935), *Women of India* (Baig ; 1958) which reflect the high aspirations of women at the time. They are written by an elite class of women and as such contain the concerns of that class of society. Entering the phase of development after Independence, the writings centre largely on women's participation in the work-force with repercussions on her social role. These studies cover a wide spectrum of women in the work force of urban areas. In the march towards development women's economic participation has assumed greater importance.

The Report of the Committee on the Status of Women in India entitled *Towards Equality* (1974) is the first major attempt to review

*Beteille (1966), Jacob-George (1967), Gangrade, (1974), Mehta, S.R. (1972), Narain (1976), Punit (1973), Ranganath (1974), Sirsikar (1970), Singh (1973), UNESCO (1968). (Refer Appendix).

and evaluate data on women's roles, rights and opportunities in the wake of planned development (Mazumdar ; 1979 : 116). There has been a substantial coverage of women in urban and rural areas. The Committee on the Status of Women does not favour special reservation of seats at the State and National levels but strongly recommends the provisions of special opportunities for representation at the local Government level (1974 : 372). The Committee suggests the establishment of Statutory Women's Panchayats in the hope that women may be able to participate more effectively through this channel. These women's panchayats can send representatives to the Zilla Parishad and Panchayat Samiti. The Report of the Committee on Panchayati Raj Institutions (1978 : 141) suggests having an institutional arrangement through a Committee with all women members of the Mandal Panchayat represented on it. This body is meant to ensure that decision are made by women themselves on priorities and choices in welfare and development programmes specifically for women and children.

The latest publication *Symbols of Power*, edited by Vina Muzumdar (SNDT, 1979) contains several studies on the political status of women in various States of the country. The populations covered are generally from urban areas with a sprinkling of rural women. The general view is that women in India are showing signs of political awakening but that their progress is hindered by social handicaps such as illiteracy, cultural norms, domestic pressures, dependency of men. By and large, the few women who have emerged significantly into political prominence are those who are "economically well-off" and who belong to the upper strata of society. (Muni ; 1979 : 42). A few references to women in Panchayati Raj Institutions state that statutory provision has been made for their representation in those States where no such provision had been made. The overwhelming majority of women are found to be nominated. Hardly any women stand for elections, the exceptions being found mainly at the gram panchayat level where there are several examples of women becoming 'sarpanchas' (head of the gram panchayat).

The recommendations of the Committee on the Status of Women as well as the Report of the Committee on Panchayati Raj institutions reflect a concern to have all women's bodies thus making women more responsible for their own development. It is necessary before one reaches the stage of making suggestions, to study the actual composition, the thinking and participation of women on these bodies in order to assess the realistic possibilities inherent in the situation.

Andrea Singh (1975 : 217, 218) in commenting on methodology regarding studies of women in India finds that the studies have not had sufficient reference to actual behaviour and careful delineation of the relevance of important social/cultural variables such as religion, caste, region, family structures or systems of kinship and marriage. She goes on to point out that such knowledge is essential for the understanding of the special problems of women in Indian society and would seem to be a pre-requisite for arriving at solutions and policy decisions meant to alleviate these problems and to create an atmosphere of greater equality.

The present study is an attempt to study socio-economic and cultural factors in the background of women-members of the PS/ZP in order to see their relevance in the present pattern and their expected role performance.

2

METHODOLOGY

GENERAL AIM OF THE STUDY

THE aim of the study is to explore the social background that characterises the women-members of Zilla Parishads and Panchayat Samitis in order to discover the factors that may determine their social participation. The ultimate aim of Panchayati Raj is to involve the local community, hence local women, in the process of development. In order to initiate the involvement of local women, one has to take note of the socio-cultural context in which they live, its influences on their thought and action. In exploring this background, one will be able to also assess how best women-members have been able to make their social contribution through panchyat structures. Being a new area of study one has to start by asking broad questions about the nature of their participation and the factors that help or hinder the social responses of women-members.

SCOPE OF THE STUDY

The scope of the present study may be understood more clearly by a preliminary brief discussion of the administrative set-up in Panchayati Raj.

The Balwantrai Mehta Committee (1959) recommended "the setting up of the elected and organically linked democratic bodies at the village, block and district levels" which would be entrusted with "planning and development activities hitherto done at the State level". (Jacob; 1970 : v). The States were left free to follow the administrative pattern most suited to the region, provided that the basic objective of transferring power to the people was respected.

The directives given by the Centre were studied by the Government of Maharashtra through the Naik Committee (1961) of which the major recommendations were accepted. These recommendations led to the setting up of a three-tier system: the Zilla Parishad (ZP) for the district, the Panchayat Samiti (PS) for the block in addition to the already established Gram Panchayat (GP) for the village. The system of Panchayati Raj envisaged a three-tier system with autonomous and elective bodies at the district, taluka and village levels, but Maharashtra opted for a system whereby only the ZP and GP would be autonomous and elective bodies; the middle-tier body *i.e.* the Panchayat Samiti would function as an executive committee of the ZP (Government of Maharashtra; 1971 : 11). Thus, "the Zilla Parishads have been conceived as the mainstay of the whole system . . . . All the powers have been concentrated in the hands of the Zilla Parishad . . . . The P.S. and G.P. act as agents of the Z.P." (Sirsikar; 1970 : 8).

The composition of each of these three bodies has been laid down according to statutory requirements as contained in the Maharashtra Zilla Parishad and Panchayat Samiti Act of 1961 and the Bombay Village Panchayat Act of 1968. A statutory representation of women has been provided on each of the bodies at the district, block and village levels.

The present study has chosen to focus attention only on women in the Panchayat Samitis and Zilla Parishads of Maharashtra. Women in the Gram Panchayats have not been included in the sample. Being a pioneer-study of women in Panchayati Raj, it was thought necessary to extend the range of the study so as to gain a general view of the situation in the State. To include women in Gram Panchayats, it would have been necessary to limit the area of investigation because of the large numbers of women at the village level.

The study has thus confined itself to the Zilla Parishads and Panchayat Samitis of 24 rural districts of Maharashtra.* Only one district was excluded, that of Nasik, because the ZP and PS had been superseded in August 1975 and an Administrator appointed on behalf of the Government. All women who had been elected or co-opted as members of the ZP or PS of the districts of Maharashtra and who

*The study was conducted before the division of the districts of Ratnagiri, Aurangabad, Osmanabad, and Chandrapur which brings the present total number of rural districts to 30.

held office for the term during which the study was conducted were eligible to be included in the sample and came within the scope of the study.

SPECIFIC OBJECTIVES OF THE STUDY

The specific objectives of the study follow from the general aim which is to see how far women's role on the ZP/PS accords with the expected role and the factors that may help or stand in the way of her expected functioning. The study starts by asking: Who are the representatives among women ? What is their background ? What do they think about social issues in general and those concerning women in particular ? What are they able to do as members of the ZP/PS ?

The objectives may, therefore, be spelled out as :

(a) to study the socio-economic and political background of elected or nominated women-representatives on the ZP/PS;

(b) to study the social outlook and awareness of women-members in regard to women's role in society, including broadly the areas of education, employment, marriage, family;

(c) to find out the scope and extent of women-member's participation in activities of the ZP/PS as well as in development activity concerning women in particular and the rural community as a whole;

(d) to find out the factors which may help or prevent women from playing a more effective role through the ZP/PS.

THE SETTING OF THE STUDY

The selection of Maharashtra as the State in which to conduct the study was based on the following considerations :

(a) Maharashtra is one of the States where the experiment of Panchayati Raj has been found to have worked most successfully. It is attributed to the stability of the administrative set-up which also results from a cohesive political structure such as existed till 1977. The report of the

Committee on Panchayati Raj institutions (1978: 4) makes the following comments about P.S. functioning in Maharashtra : " . . . . the first point of decentralisation at the district level, was organised in Maharashtra and Gujarat and it has functioned effectively, particularly in the field of decentralised planning and development." Again, the report (p. 8) says that wherever Panchayati Raj institutions have been given the responsibility of development to whatever limited extent, as in Maharashtra and Gujarat, they have done well.

(b) The researcher was more familiar with the physical layout of Maharashtra than that of any other State. This was a helpful consideration since the researcher had to travel alone over vast rural areas. Contact persons were known in different districts who helped make arrangements for boarding and lodging. Familiarity with the language enabled the researcher to interview every respondent personally.

SAMPLING

As a first step in the process of selecting the sample, it was felt that the universe could be stratified according to the regional divisions of the State. The four regions of Maharashtra are ;

1. Vidarbha,
2. Marathwada,
3. Pune Division,
4. Bombay Division.

The Pune-Bombay Divisions are also now as the Western Region. A region-wise stratification of the sample would render the process of data-collection in each region more convenient because of a certain administrative unity. Moreover each region has a historical past, distinct geographical features and a certain pattern of socio-economic development which exercise a particular influence on women's social emergence in the region. This may enable one to make some generalisations or at least draw attention to the interplay of certain specific variables on women's social development. This study, being at a first stage of exploration, the researcher preferred to have a broad view of the subject without any prior assumptions about women's performance in PR. It was assumed that the data collected in the field would itself allow issues to emerge, at times more clearly, at other times obscurely, but the interest was to see the issues that are of importance to the rural woman, as they emerge in direct contact with her.

To give greater validity to the findings of the study, it was felt that a sample including fifty per cent of the population of women in the ZP/PS of the region would better serve the purpose. It was difficult to draw an absolute line between ZP councillors and PS members because all ZP councillors automatically become members of the PS of their taluka of residence in addition to the co-opted PS member. In several cases they were the only women representatives in the PS of their taluka. This is also the reason why the ZP and PS representatives have been treated as one group for the investigation. There was no need of administering different sets of questions.

The population of the women-members of the ZP/PS for each region was calculated mainly on the basis of information supplied from the ZP office in each district. Each ZP is expected to have at least two women-members and each PS at least one. The total population for each region was found to be as follows :

Vidarbha	:	118	women-members
Marathwada	:	53	,, ,,
Pune Division	:	78	,, ,,
Bombay Division	:	71	,, ,,
Total		320	

Having obtained the population for each region, it was proposed to take a sample of 50 per cent of the regional population, observing as far as possible the same proportion in the districts. The district-wise stratification and calculation (of 50 per cent) yielded the following sample :

1.	Vidarbha	:	56	women-members
2.	Marathwada	:	25	,, ,,
3.	Pune Division	:	38	,, ,,
4.	Bombay Division	:	34	,, ,,
	Total.........		153	

In order that each region have as representative a sample as possible of the component districts, every effort was made to observe the district-variations in the regional sample.

At first it was proposed to select the respondents in each district by means of a random sample. However, this plan had to be abandoned in view of the following difficulties :

1. The choice of a random sample would necessitate a complete list of women-members of the district in advance. This type of information was not possible to obtain from all the districts. A personal visit would have been necessary to Zilla Parishad offices and it was hardly possible to envisage a visit in the district areas just for this information, given the limitations of time and cost involved.
2. Even if it was possible to choose a random sample, the next question would be : where does the woman reside and is it possible to reach her house by State Transport Bus Service or would one need to make special arrangements? Besides there was no assurance of finding the woman at her residence even after travelling the distance.
3. The question of advance information about the researcher's visit to the respondent's home could forestall some difficulties but it was not possible to expect all ZP offices to intimate the address of all the women-members from their districts. Moreover, with the difficulty of transport and communication in villages, there was no guarantee that the letters would reach their destination nor that replies would be received in the time available. An important factor to foresee was that women in rural areas would hardly be in a position to understand the import of a research conveyed in a letter and that such communication may have proved to be more of a liability than an asset for the research.

For all the above reasons, it became obvious that selection by random sampling was not feasible. The next alternative was that the researcher would have to personally visit each district centre and see what arrangement could be made so that the number of women-members in the proposed district sample could be interviewed. The following procedure was adopted.

1. Advance information was sent to the Chief Executive Officer (CEO) of each district explaining the purpose of the visit and the proposed number of interviewees required in the district. The CEO was requested to make contacts with the BDOs of the Panchayat Samitis to be selected. The selection of the women-members was left to the discretion of the concerned CEO or the Dy. CEO in consultation with the BDO of the particular area. Since the researcher depended very much on their help for contacting the women and travelling to remote village areas situated beyond the network of State Transport Services, she had to fit the demands of the sample with the possibilities of time and transport available at the ZP/PS offices. The visits to villages by official transport had to be chalked out on the basis of convenience of district officials for example, if an extension officer or other staff member had a tour programme in a particular area covering two or three blocks, the researcher would benefit by his visit to contact the women-members of the ZP/PS residing in those areas.
2. The interviews were arranged to be held preferably at the residence of the members in most of the cases but as time was limited and transport not easy to arrange, towards the latter part of data-collection, members were requested to meet the researcher at the Samiti Office which is usually a more accessible place.

After 8 months of data-collection, having visited 24 districts of Maharashtra, the researcher was able to interview 144 out of the proposed sample of 153 women members.

TABLE 2.1 : **A view of the actual sample obtained**

Region	District	Proposed sample	Actual sample
1. Vidarbha	Buldhana	7	6
	Akola	7	6
	Amravati	7	6
	Nagpur	7	8
	Bhandara	7	6
	Wardha	4	6
	Yavatmal	8	8
	Chandrapur	9	8
	Total	56	54

TABLE 2.1—*contd.*

Region	District	Proposed sample	Actual sample
2. Marathwada	Aurangabad	7	7
	Parbhani	5	5
	Beed	4	3
	Nanded	3	3
	Osmanabad	6	4
	Total	25	22
3. Pune Division	Ahmednagar	6	5
	Pune	7	5
	Satara	7	5
	Sholapur	7	7
	Sangli	4	6
	Kolhapur	7	7
	Total	38	35
4. Bombay Division	Thane	7	7
	Kolaba	7	7
	Ratnagiri	7	5
	Nasik (excluded)	—	—
	Dhule	7	8
	Jalgaon	6	6
	Total	34	33
	Total of 4 regions	153	144

Table 2.1 shows that the shortfall in each region ranges between 1 and 3 respondents. Sometimes the number interviewed in a district goes a little higher than the proposed sample because it was easier to contact women-members in those districts and the researcher had to obtain the number required for the total regional sample. It was comparatively easier to travel in the smaller districts like Wardha and Sangli. Wherever transport was easily available, even far-flung talukas in Aurangabad or Dhule, were possible to visit.

DATA COLLECTION

The period of data collection was indeed a period of challenge for the researcher, an adventure into the unknown, the discovery of a vibrant reality that pulsates beneath the slow rhythm and utter simplicity of rural surroundings.

In most cases, the CEOs and BDOs as well as the officials in the ZP/PS were very co-operative and often went out of their way to help the researcher reach remote village areas which would have otherwise been out of the pale of the study. It was not easy to fix a programme for the researcher within the limited space of 4 or 5 days in several blocks of the district and that with short notice. For reasons already mentioned it was not possible to fix even the semblance of an itinerary in advance. It may be of interest to list some of the situations that the researcher had to take in her stride during the process of data-collection.

1. In places where the CEO might have been away from the headquarters, the next in command would not know what is expected to be done for **a** 'non-official', 'a student', 'a lady' travelling alone.
2. At times one would reach the residence of the respondent, happy at having been able to make it, only to find that the respondent just happened to have gone to a relative's place some distance away.
3. A few times because of the monsoon, the village was not accessible by any form of transport.
4. Sometimes the office phone as a means of advance contact, was found not working repeatedly for 2 or 3 days and so the facilities for an overnight halt in the place to be visited could not be fixed.

One incident may reveal the difficulties faced in data collection during the monsoon in the rural setting. The researcher had informed officials at the ZP office of a district (J) that she would be visiting the district in order to interview a few women-members from there. On arrival she found that no programme had been drawn up and that she would have to mark time in trying to make appointments. A meeting of Block Development Officers was in session at the ZP office and the researcher sought permission to enquire whether appointment could be made with the women-members of their Panchayat Samitis. Nothing could be done immediately, but interviews were arranged for the following week. Meanwhile the researcher had to turn to an adjacent district where contacts were somewhat easier. She returned to district (J) after four days and got the ZP office to trunk call a particular BDO, reminding him of her appointed visit to his Samiti office. On the day fixed, the researcher had difficulty to get an State

Transport bus to the area concerned because of the continuous downpour of rain. She left at 7 A.M. by one bus, then had to change into another which took a longer route on a more motorable road. The Samiti office was at a distance of about 40 kilometres from the District headquarters. On reaching the Samiti office at 1 P.M., the researcher was told that the member was not able to come as she had to manage her shop in the village. She was a widow and probably had to work hard for her family. The BDO had been good enough to send two of his staff members the previous evening to inform the member about the researcher's visit and since she requested that the researcher should come to her place, the BDO decided that he would give his jeep for the purpose. Thus, when the researcher arrived at the Samiti office, all was in readiness to leave : the staff members accompanying the researcher, the driver and jeep. The jeep started while it was still raining and drove on midst slush and the ruggedness of rain-washed paths. The slush, especially the black, clayey soil was a constant deterrent to the wheels. Suddenly the jeep was stuck......nothing could make it go. Driver, passers-by, all tucked up their sleeves and started pushing. A cartoonist would have revealed in viewing the whole situation but the researcher was ridden with only one quest : to interview the woman-member. Once again, after much effort, the jeep was on its way. It turned into a road......or was it a river ! It was impossible to continue driving the vehicle through so much water......The driver shook his head......no way of proceeding either by vehicle or on foot. Thirty-eight kilometres of difficult travel and just when the member was hardly 2 kilometres away, the researcher had to reconcile herself to the impossibility of contacting her for about 2 days. The researcher left the Samiti office sorely disappointed, yet was cordially invited to visit again after the rains.

The period of data collection took a little over 8 months from a March-summer to the end of the monsoon in October, travelling through the hot winds of Dhule and Akola, refreshed by the bracing cool, hilly air of Kolhapur, Sangli, Buldhana : up the misty climbs of Ratnagiri, overlooking a chess-board of fresh greenery to the flat, dry stretches of Sholapur and eventually, the thick, dark hush of the Chandrapur forest. One had to be prepared for whatever board and lodging could be found : whether in the unknown walls of a guest house, the warmth of a convent or the simple set-up of a village homestead. For travel, the researcher had to rely mainly on State Transport buses besides the sympathetic response from ZP officials who offered the facility of an office jeep.

For the city-bred researcher, the miles and miles of travel in wide rural expanses was a discovery indeed......a discovery of the immensity of the rural area and the problems of its vast, sprawling population. Facilities for transport and communication being insufficient, many parts of rural India continue to remain isolated and cut off from the mainstream. The procurement of water, especially drinking water, poses quite a challenge particularly in the hot season. However, an effort is on, slow though it be, to ameliorate existing conditions. The system of Panchayati Raj has managed to generate a ripple of interest among the people to use opportunities available for the use of power as also for services required.

The charm of the rural set-up lies in its proverbial hospitality. They lose no time in rolling out the red carpet for visitors. Their constant appeals : "Sit down, have a cup of tea !", "What if you wait till tomorrow ?", "When will you come again" ?, brought home to the researcher the warmth of rural communities graced by a sense of the 'personal'—as against the anxiety of the researcher to get on with a task !

TOOLS OF DATA COLLECTION

The main tool of data collection was the interview-schedule. Each interviewee was met personally by the researcher who tried to conduct the interview in the homes of the respondents, so as to arrive at a better understanding of their social environment.

Some parts of the schedule contained questions, the responses to which were coded in advance. This applies specially to the section on the socio-economic background of respondents. The sections exploring social outlook and awareness as well as the social participation of respondents were left open-ended.

At the start, the researcher had tried to devise four-point scales to explore attitudes towards certain situations but the very first interviews in Thana District exposed the wide disparity that exists among the respondents in terms of education, exposure to change and social class. It was difficult to frame questions to suit an illiterate tribal woman engaged in agricultural occupation, and the graduate housewife engaged in a variety of social service activities at the local, district or State levels. The administration of scales was not found to be helpful in indicating the responses of the members hence the question-answer form was preferred.

STATISTICAL ANALYSIS

Cross-tabulations have been used frequently to observe possibly significant relations between independent variables like age, education, caste, land-holdings, political influence and dependent variables like social outlook and social participation. The χ^2 test has been used to establish the significance of the relationship between most variables. The gamma test of correlation was used to indicate the degree of interdependence between variables. Qualitative analysis was found to be more effective in describing the opinions held on social issues as contained in Chapter 4.

LIMITATIONS OF THE STUDY

As earlier explained, it was not possible to obtain the exact number of respondents as indicated by the proposed sample, nor was it possible to select them randomly. The actual sample was selected according to the advice of the administrative staff of ZP offices.

A study in a rural area may need more time for participant-observation and in this sense the present study was somewhat hurried. The setting was too extensive to be covered in the period of time specified for the thesis. The insecurity of having to stay in unknown places made the researcher hurry the period of data-collection which often reduced contacts with the rural respondents to a quick one-hour question-answer session. In some places having to depend on the transport offered by officials one had to follow their schedule and so to sandwitch interviews as best as possible between schedules. People from village areas were anxious to meet the researcher and talk but the researcher was often constrained to keep time mainly for interviews with the respondent and thus perhaps miss some of the richness of the cultural context. The absence of any transport facility other than State Transport bus service also led to considerable delays in the daily schedule of work. For further studies on women in Panchayati Raj, it may be better to limit the scope of the study to a more circumscribed area and include women in the Gram Panchayat as well. A wider spectrum of levels of social participation among women would possibly emerge and thus permit more valid generalisations. Limitations of the area could also permit a richer understanding of women's position by contact with other people concerned in the area of exploration.

The researcher limited the investigation only to women members on ZP/PS. There was no objective verification of the information given e.g. awareness of services actually existing in the areas where members resided or claims on the part of members to social participation. It may be of help to study the perception of officials and non-officials of women's role in PR, and to observe participation patterns in actual situations e.g. at a ZP meeting.

The present study has focussed attention only on the women-members; their background, their social outlook and social participation. It is their perception of their own status and performance that is the object of study.

3

SOCIO-ECONOMIC BACKGROUND OF THE WOMEN-MEMBERS IN PANCHAYAT INSTITUTIONS

INTRODUCTION

KNOWLEDGE of the socio-economic background of a community is an indispensable prerequisite for the understanding of the thought or behaviour of its members. This holds good for all human communities, and more so in the case of rural communities which are intrinsically more traditional in their structure. Traditions tend to be observed with rigidity and family as well as caste status play an important role in directing the course of life for the individual. (Desai; 1969 : 33). If the above is generally true of all members of rural communities, it is even more so in the life of the rural woman for whom every step in life is ritually prescribed, leaving a rather small margin for personal choice. Altekar (1938 : 394-395) explains that Manu's injunction to the father that he ought to protect a woman while she is a maiden, the husband when she has married, and the sons when the husband is no more, was motivated primarily to give woman the protection she needed. In the course of time the phrase came to be construed in a literal sense with the understanding that a woman deserves no independence, that she ought not to do anything on her own initiative right from her childhood, youth, and even in old age. Thus woman come to occupy an increasingly dependent position in the family. Unexposed to social pressures outside the home, the power of family influence tends to get intensified in her case. In todays' world family prestige and status are judged according to that of senior male members because they play an important part in the occupational, religious and legal systems of society. They are the considered representatives of the family. A woman is allotted the prestige and status of her husband or father-in-law (Ward; 1963 : 97).

Women in rural areas enjoy for the most part, an ascriptive status, which means that it is necessary to study the status of father and husband in order to appreciate the social position of the rural woman. In spite of the change that is affecting the social structure of rural communities, women are still very much under the power of the family. The rural family which is in most cases an agricultural household, is characterised by a greater closeness among its members and thus more liable to be influenced by hereditary traits and family culture. The family is, therefore, the most important influence in the life of the rural woman who is usually confined to the home. The changes that are affecting the features of rural society are experienced by the woman through her family. The economic, political and social involvement of the family is the atmosphere in which the thought and aspirations of the woman are nourished and given shape.

However, the traditional influence of the family is now gradually being offset by other forces at work in rural society. These forces have come into play with the setting up of democratic organisations such as that of Panchayati Raj. The structure of Panchayati Raj has incorporated the ideal of equality in development, riding over traditional barriers of caste and class to make way for freer participation and greater social mobility among rural communities. In Maharashtra it is twenty years since the provision for statutory representation of women has been made on panchayat bodies. Given the traditional past in which rural women have grown up and the process of social change generated by these new channels of development, it is of interest to view the new role that women-members of the panchayat are called upon to play and the manner in which they respond to the challenge. This study seeks to do this in the context of the socio-economic profile of these new "representatives" of rural women. The questions that will be studied in this chapter are :

(1) From which caste-group and class are the respondents drawn ?

(2) What kind of family background do the respondents have in terms of parents' or husbands' education, occupation and socio-political involvement ?

(3) What is the personal background of the respondent in terms of her marital status, family responsibility, education and social activity ?

These questions will be studied under three heads:

A. Parental Household
B. Husband's Household
C. Personal Background of Respondent.

PARENTAL HOUSEHOLD

In order to view the social, economic and political influence in the parental home, the following items were investigated:

(a) Caste and Caste-group
(b) Father's occupation
(c) Father's education
(d) Mother's education
(e) Family participation in socio-political activity.

Caste and caste-group

"Caste largely determines the function, the status, the available opportunities as well as the handicaps for an individual" (Desai ; 1969 : 38). The influence of caste is well marked in rural society. In the following Table 3.1 the broad distinctions of caste-groups will be used with specific mention of the numerically dominant castes that compose each division.

TABLE 3.1 : Distribution of respondents according to caste-groups

Caste-Groups			No. of Respondents	Percentage
1. Advanced castes (Brahmin)			12	8
3. Intermediate castes :			99	69
Maratha Kshatriya	59	] 74	51	
Maratha Kunbi	15			
Gujar, Leva Patil	4			
Lingayat	11			
Migrant Settlers	3			
Marwadi	2			
Non-Hindus (Jain, Jew, Muslim)	5			
	99			
3. Backward castes (Artisan and Service castes—dhangar, mali, teli, nhavi, dhobi, koshti)			20	
4. Scheduled castes/Scheduled tribes (mahar, warli, bhil, gond)			13	9
Total			144	100

From the above classification, it is seen that 99 (about 69%) respondents come from the Intermediate castes which consist of a majority (74/144) of Maratha Kshatriya and Maratha Kunbis. Enthoven (1975 : 8) says that the word 'Maratha' covers three groups that were probably one in origin but are now distinct :

(1) Marathas Proper. They are the chiefs, landowners and fighting Marathas of the Deccan and Konkan claiming Kshatriya rank.
(2) Maratha Kunbis or cultivators.
(3) Maratha occupational castes such as Bhandari, Kumbhar, Lohar, Mali, Nhavi, Sutar, Teli.

In the Table 3.1 the third group of occupational castes has been listed in with Caste-group 3 : Backward Castes. For the present study, the term Maratha has been applied to the Maratha Kshatriya and Kunbi groups, which constitute the numerically dominant castes. Sirsikar (1970 : 40) estimates the Maratha caste group at 40 per cent of the population of Maharashtra, which means that their presence among women in PS/ZP (51%) is far more than their actual proportion in the population of the State.

Among the specific caste-groups mentioned in Table 3.1, the Maratha Kshatriya group is the largest. It was with a sense of pride that respondents affirmed their belonging to the "Shivaji Maratha", "Rajgharana" or "Rajput" group. The region-wise sample distribution in percentage form of this particular caste-group is as follows :

Vidarbha : 33 per cent, Marathwada 45 per cent, Pune Division 57 per cent and Bombay Division 30 per cent. The Pune Division is thus the stronghold of the Shivaji Maratha. Formerly, they were chiefs and rulers, representing a rural aristocracy and so were conservative, intensely proud and largely illiterate. Many of the respondents belonging to this group related how strictly they had been brought up as women, hardly allowed to attend school, having to observe *purdah* (veil) and never appearing before men without their heads and faces covered. The Marathas owned lands as feudal lords. Among the "royal" Marathas, the women folk were confined to their homes and however poor, they never worked on the land. (Karve ; 1968 : 76). Thus we may say that 41 per cent of the respondents in the sample belong to the rural aristocracy with a very protected family background.

The next important single caste-group from the numerical standpoint, is that of the Maratha Kunbi, "the great agricultural caste of the Maratha country". (Russell ; 1975 : 16). Out of the 15 respondents, 14 are found in the Vidarbha region. They belong to the proprietory and cultivating communities and were mostly illiterate. Many of the leading families in Vidarbha today belong to the Kunbi community.

In examining the rural social structure in countries of Southern Asia, the UNESCO Research Centre (1968) has the following analysis to make about India :

> ......There were regionally dominant castes, occupying a dominant economic status and owning most of the land, who did not belong to the highest status in the caste hierarchy. While the land-owners are generally of higher castes in Indian villages, it is their position as land owners rather than caste membership *per se* which gives them status and power. Even Brahmins who occupy top positions in the orthodox Hindu scale may not be influential in a village because they are economically dependent.

Table 3.1 shows that the Brahmins count for only 8 per cent of the representation. The Leva Patil and Gujar respondents who count for 3 per cent of the sample and who belong to the Intermediate castes are also part of the important agricultural castes, who generally have a dominant economic status.

M.S. Gore (1968 : 54, 55) describing the general attributes of Indian rural leaders, says that "on the attribute of caste the leader should belong to the dominant caste which is usually the most numerous and economically dominant caste-group". The concept of the dominant caste has two components : numerical domination and economic domination. Where the same caste is dominant in both these aspects its power and claim to leadership is unquestioned. In spite of new trends that are taking place in rural leadership, through the introduction of democratic institutions based on election, it must be recognised that membership of the dominant caste is an important criterion for acquiring leadership. The history of village organisation in Maharashtra shows that each village had its "Headman" or "Patil" who was an important landholder and a hereditary chief. The Patilship is generally the privilege of Maratha families. The office of 'Patil' was two-fold : the Mulki Patil collected the revenue and the Police Patil looked after the law and order situation (Karve ; 1968 : 148). Many Maratha respondents came from these families. Such is also the case of the Kunbi village headmen who bear the name of Deshmukh (Russell ; 1975 : 17).

It is seen that numerical superiority, high land-owning status and traditional positions of authority give to the Maratha (Kshatriya and Kunbi) group the status of the dominant caste in Maharashtra and it is from this complex that the largest number of women representatives on Panchayat Samitis and Zilla Parishad are selected.

The Scheduled Castes (SC) and Scheduled Tribes (ST) constitute 9 per cent of the sample whereas the estimate of the SC/ST population given by the Census of Maharashtra, 1971, is 12 per cent of the total population. This indicates a proportionately lower level of representation for the SC/ST group which is known to be an under-privileged group socially, as well as economically. It is interesting to note the regionwise distribution in the sample as against the regional distribution of SC/ST in the Census of Maharashtra, 1971.

TABLE 3.2 : **Region-wise distribution of SC/ST in sample and SC/ST population in Maharashtra**

		Vidarbha	Marathwada	Pune Division	Bombay Division
Proportion of SC	in M'tra State	4.34	10.18	9.45	2.71
	in sample	3.70	4.54	0.00	0.00
Proportion of ST	in M'tra State	5.68	2.00	2.64	20.70
	in sample	3.70	0.00	0.00	18.80

Note : The 'sample' figures quoted in the above table, represent the SC who occupy the reserved seats for women, on PS/ZP bodies

Source : Census 1971—Maharashtra : General Population Tables; p. 210.

Table 3.2 shows that the proportion of SC/ST members is markedly below the actual population figures. What is still more striking is the absence of SC in the Pune Division and a very low representation in Marathwada both of which have the highest concentration of SC and the highest concentration of the Maratha Kshatriya caste group. One may raise a question about the exercise of power and control by the dominant group to the detriment of those who have a low ritual as well as social status. The Bombay Division and Vidarbha have a lower concentration of the Maratha Kshatriya group and a higher proportion of representation accorded to the SC/ST groups. The researcher was able to sense a certain amount of tension between the Intermediate class groups and the SC/ST groups, but the resentment was directed more against the SC. The period of data collection in Marathwada coincided with the visit of the Enquiry Commission set up to investigate the cause of the tension and riots as a sequel to a proposal to rename the Marathwada University, as Ambedkar University. In informal discussion, Maratha respondents expressed their fear that this may lead to a complete take over of the University by the SC ; the educational privileges and concessions extended to SC were lowering standards in professional practice. Their children who had performed better, were being left out to make room for underserving candidates—so they felt. In some districts, resentment was expressed by respondents from the land-owning classes against the agricultural labourers demanding higher wages. As a result of scarce labour the crops suffered and the yield of land had diminished. The opinion expressed by Srinivas (1976 ; 211) regarding the village of Rampura, could also be applied in this situation :

> It could also be safely presumed that the members of the higher castes, and in particular, the locally dominant caste, were opposed to land passing into the hands of the lowest castes who provided the main source of agricultural labour.

The respondents reflect the tension and attitude that characterise the milieu to which they belong and this is important to note because they occupy a position of formal leadership in panchayat bodies.

Among the SC/ST respondents, two belong to agricultural labour households. They are the only representatives of female agricultural labour though the percentage of this group to the total population is 13.68 per cent as compared with cultivators who form only 9.28 per cent of the total population. In the sample, the majority of respondents belong to the high land-owning class where it is a matter of prestige that women do not work on the land. If these women representatives have to contribute towards women's development in rural society, they cannot ignore the needs and problems of women in agricultural labour. The question arises whether members having the social background as described, can pay the required attention to these socially disadvantaged sectors of women.

The unequal representation as seen above, should not, however, blind one to 'signs of promise' heralded by the statutory representation of women on panchayat bodies. These signs may be enumerated as :

1. Out of the 13 SC/ST respondents, 8 are tribal women and 3 belong to the Mang and Mahar castes. Two of the latter call themselves Nav Buddh. In the traditional rural social structure the SC/ST may never have been admitted into the hallowed circles of caste panchayats, least of all women of these castes, but today democratic forms of development have permitted the illiterate tribal or Dhobi caste woman to sit beside the 'royal' Maratha to become more conscious of the larger community of which they are a part.
2. The researcher interviewed a respondent (PS member) in Marathwada, who belonged to a backward class group and lived in a village predominantly inhabited by people of the Mang caste. The people of this village had been able to form their own Gram Panchayat for the first time and since the respondent was the most educated woman in the village, they selected her to be the woman representative. She was keen on working for the benefit of the village and sought the help of the researcher, by writing to her later in order to get an approach road as well as facilities for a balwadi in their village.
3. Another bright spark of change was observed on visiting the home of a respondent, a Brahmin lady in Vidarbha, who had employed a Harijan girl to fill water and work in their kitchen.
4. An adivasi PS member was the first successful SC candidate in her taluka ; she was continuing studies at the B.A. level and was in charge of an Adivasi Trust for Youth.

The fact that all the classes and castes of women have been able to find a new identity as representatives with equal status, able to participate in the work of Panchayat bodies which affect the whole rural community is certainly a step forward.

The group of Brahmin respondents is fairly equally distributed in all the four divisions. Among the districts, Ratnagiri has the highest number in the sample, since 3 out of the 5 interviewees from that district are Brahmins. They form about 6 per cent of the population in Maharashtra (Karve ; 1968 : 76) and count for 8 per cent of the sample, a somewhat proportionate representation.

The other categories in Table 3.1 include, Lingayats, Marwadis, two settlers from Gujarat (one in agriculture, the other in a cloth selling business), a refugee settler from the Punjab, a Jew, Jain and Muslim. Some of these have settled in Maharashtra for generations but a few had settled just one generation earlier. They have integrated themselves into the local way of life, speaking Marathi and educating their children in Marathi medium schools. The local community has accepted them and has even shown confidence by selecting them to be representatives on the PS and ZP. These particular respondents belong to minority groups in the taluka. Their economic status is good being traders in one or other commercial activity. The question of caste and religion has not come in the way of their integration with the community. A particular case in point is that of an illiterate Punjabi respondent in the Pune Division. She and her husband came as refugees after Independence and settled in a remote village, where they started a cloth selling business Their successful business enabled the husband to acquire some land and not having kith or kin in the new surroundings they became closely identified with the local population, especially with the less privileged sections of the area. Thus her husband was elected to the Z.P. Upon her husband's untimely death, the people voted the wife into the seat of Councillor on the Zilla Parishad and she proved herself equal to the task—an extraordinary achievement for a woman in rural society and a testimony to the receptivity of the local population. While the case above serves to demonstrate the effectiveness of democratic participation in furthering the cause of development, there are other cases where caste and group rivalry militate against the aspiration of development. In a particular village visited by the researcher, a young educated Brahmin girl tried to start a balwadi and some group activities for women. Intense rivalry among the less educated caste groups (Leva-Patil and Maratha) led to non co-operation among the women which finally ended in the closing of all activities for women and children. The educated Brahmin girl who could have helped in her own village looked for opportunities outside. In spite of having other educated and active women in the village, the women's representative on the Gram Panchayat as well as on the Panchayat Samiti, happened to be illiterate and socially inactive but the wife of a big land-owner belonging to the dominant caste-group in the village. This is an illustration of caste-rivalry entwined with political considerations which work against the development of women as evisaged by the status, and surely, this is not the only case of such counter-development moves.

Father's occupation

The occupation of the head of a rural household reflects the social and economic status of the parental home. The occupation of the fathers shows that over 66 per cent (96) of the fathers were cultivators. Details about the land ownership status of the fathers were not asked of the women for fear that it might get complicated for the women to answer and time would be spent on issues that were less important for this particular study. Ten of the fathers also did a supplementary job like working in the talathi's or mamlatdar's office or carried on a small business like the sale of betel nuts. Among the cultivators one respondent mentioned that her father and husband were *Jagirdars* and one said her father was an *Izzar*. In two cases, the fathers, one belonging to the SC and the other to the ST, were agricultural labourers, while all the others from the SC/ST group belonged to the upper economic strata of their own caste or tribal group. Their average property ranged between 5-10 acres. Among those engaged in cottage industry, or having a small business there was a weaver, tailor, dhobi, a gold-seller, a hotel manager and those having *kirana* or cloth shops.

Service occupations account for 17 per cent of the sample. These range from the job of a sepoy or mill-worker to a garrison engineer and they generally expose the person concerned to a greater measure of urban influence since the location of work is an office, factory or a work establishment in the taluks headquarters or city. Professions account for a very small percentage of the sample and among these, teaching is the most widely practised.

From the angle of agricultural/non-agricultural occupation, it is seen that 96 or two-thirds of the fathers were engaged in agricultural production and there is a concentration of these in Marathwada and Vidarbha. Bombay and Pune Divisions have the greater concentration of non-agricultural occupations, which characterise an urbanised society.

Father's education

Education did not figure high in the socio-cultural life of the land-owning classes. However, after compulsory education has become one of the Directive Principles of the Constitution, and its need recognised in an evolving society, more people are using the facilities provided. The education of the parents is an indication of the process of social change that is taking place in the respondents' families. The following is a table showing the educational level of the parents.

TABLE 3.3 : **Educational level of parents**

Level of Education	No. of Father	Per cent	No. of Mother	Per cent
1. Illiterate	35	24	104	72
2. Primary	43	30	26	18
3. Middle	36	25	11	8.4
4. Secondary	16	11	2	1
5. Undergraduate	2	1.5	—	—
6. Graduate	2	1.5	—	—
7. Post-graduate/Prof. degree	4	3.0	1	0.6
8. Don't know	6	4.0	—	—
Total	144	100.0	144	100.0

Fathers

The data above shows a high percentage (76) of literate and educated fathers as against 24 per cent who belong to the illiterate category. Of the literate and educated group, the largest number (30%) have had education up to the primary level and 25 per cent up to the middle school. The 17 per cent (24 fathers) who have had education up to and beyond the secondary level have lived or boarded in district or city surroundings because at the time of their education, there were very few high schools in villages and colleges were located in a few urban centres.

Those who could go for education beyond the primary and secondary levels would have to belong to families with a comparatively higher socio-economic status considering the expenditure involved. Moreover, in an agricultural economy, the weaker sections would not find much purpose in the existent type of education.

Mothers

The high rate of illiteracy among the mothers of the respondents reflects the low level of education among women in the country at large. The difference in the percentage rates of illiteracy between the fathers and mothers (24 : 72) also reflects the wide gap that exists between the education of men and women in the country. In the case of the mothers too, the 9 per cent who have been able to go for middle-school education and above are those from the more affluent sectors.

It is worthwhile comparing the rates of literacy among fathers and mothers with male and female literacy rates in rural areas according to the Census of 1951. This Census includes Bombay, Saurashtra and Kutch which make it that the rates are not quite comparable with the regions that constitute present-day Maharashtra. However, the percentage of male literacy among agricultural classes in Bombay State is recorded as 25.98 and that of female literacy as 6.54. The sample of fathers and mothers shows much higher literacy rates than that of the general population. Census 1951 (p. 141) notes that "the disparity between male and female literacy among the agricultural classes was very wide". Literacy in their cases seemed to be related to socio-economic status with non-cultivating owners of land at the top and agricultural labourers at the lowest end. The present sample shows that the majority of respondents come from the sector of non-cultivating owners of land. Thus the higher level of education among the parents also testifies to their higher socio-economic level.

Engagement of family-members in socio-political activity

By socio-political activity is meant involvement in organisations of a social service, welfare, economic or political orientation.

The engagement of family members in socio-political activity reflects a certain atmosphere in the home environment which inevitably affects the members of the family. Rural households have a strong family identification which makes them rally round the cause espoused by senior relatives, especially if it is the male head of the household. Women as a rule do not participate in outside activities on their own and have less opportunity to be well informed in order to make their own judgement. They have generally to depend on the members of the family especially close male relatives in the areas of social or political activity.

When asked about the involvement of the parental family members in socio-political action 33 respondents definitely recalled that members of their family had been actively engaged in socio-political movements of the time. These are among those who are better educated and, for whom the involvement had a marked impact. The other 111 respondents could not respond clearly on this issue because for many it was an area of activity they were not familiar with. Moreover, it meant recalling situations that had happened years ago and which had already receded into obscurity for many. The researcher had to conduct the interviews within a limited period of time which did not leave much room for delving into the past. The interviewees had no idea about what the researcher was going to ask them and so they recalled only what happened to be prominent in their minds at the time of the interview.

Among the 33 respondents who had close relatives engaged in socio-political activity, some had several members of their family involved. It is mostly the male members, specially fathers and brothers, who took part but it is of interest to see that even a generation ago, there were rural women also who made their contribution in socio-political activity. Five respondents had their mothers and in one case, both mother and sister actively involved in the freedom movement, having courted imprisonment more than once ; one of the respondents specially recalled her mother's association with Kasturba Gandhi and how greatly she was influenced by the latter. Two mothers were Municipal Councillors and one had served on the Central Social Welfare Board. The activity of the three latter women show that the family, having resided in urban areas, exposed them to the experience of urban influence.

It is of further interest to observe the organisations in which family members of the respondents have been engaged. The following table indicates the broad areas of their involvement :

TABLE 3.4 : **The involvement of family-members in socio-political organisations**

Organisation	No. of Participants
1. Panchayat Bodies/Janpath Sabha/ Dt. Dev. Boards	15
2. Political Involvement	25
3. General Welfare Activity	13

The Table 3.4 shows that most of those who had any socio-political involvement at all, were involved in one way or another in political activity. Out of the 25 mentioned in Item 2, 12 were described as actively engaged in the freedom struggle and of these six are from the Bombay division. Out of the 6 elected Zilla Parishad women councillors in the State, 4 are from the Bombay division ; two other respondents from the same division occupied the posts of Sabhapati and Upsabhapati at the Panchayat Samiti level and one had the unique privilege in the State, of being the only woman president of a Zilla Parishad. Almost all these women attributed their developing interests in socio-political activity to the influence of their fathers, who had been active in the Indian National Congress, and subsequently some having also occupied positions in the State Government as ministers. It was interesting to listen to some of the respondents, recounting childhood experience of how their fathers had impressed upon them the importance of '*Samaj Seva*'. One respondent related how her father who had started a school in the village, agreed to send her to college in an urban area but insisted that she spend every holiday in the village, teaching poor children in the verandah of their house. Some recalled the enthusiasm which they used to welcome the national leaders of the freedom movement on their visits to their districts ; or a visit to Sevagram and the opportunity of listening to 'Bapuji'. These respondents recalled with emotion the days of the freedom movement when participation in the activity of the Indian National Congress was a high and noble ideal. For the researcher these historical developments were no more a matter of hearsay, but a living reality in the lives of these rural women who drew inspiration from the atmosphere of their homes and villages during India's struggle for independence. The Panchayat Statute provides an operational structure and an aspiration based on the spirit which was infused during the freedom struggle.

HUSBAND'S HOUSEHOLD

The researcher was able to elicit a more complete background of the husband's household because it was the current situation for the respondent and most of the interviews were conducted in the husband's home where there were others besides the respondent to volunteer information. The following items have been investigated :

(a) Caste
(b) Type of family
(c) Economic status of the family
  (i) Main source of income
  (ii) Extent of family holding
  (iii) Husband's main occupation.
(d) Husband's education
(e) Engagement of family-members in socio-political activity.

Caste

The majority of respondents have married into homes of the same caste as their own by birth, so the analysis for Table 3.1 on Caste and Caste-groups would apply here as well. There are only four cases of inter-caste marriage where the respondent married a man from a slightly lower caste. In such cases, the woman had a more liberal outlook and a tendency to rely more on her own resources rather than on the family. These women had comparatively higher education than the average respondent in the sample. Through exposure to a wider range of experience, they acquired self-confidence to hold their own in the rural community the members of which in turn nominated them to positions of responsibility as members of the PS/ZP. They have a social status which may be described as 'achieved' more than 'ascribed'.

Type of family

In type of family structure, one usually distinguishes between the joint and nuclear family. The joint family is associated with a traditional, agricultural society where conservatism and family status tend to dominate over individual interest. The nuclear family, more a development of a mobile, industrialised society permits of a greater degree of flexibility and self-expression among its members in spite of a certain sense of isolation in some respects.

The data shows that 81 respondents (56 per cent) come from joint families and 63 (44 per cent) from the nuclear type.

It would be expected that in a sample where the majority of respondents come from agricultural households, the greater number would live in joint families. Their percentage figures show that there is a comparatively high incidence of nuclear families. A close view of the data collected indicates that in the cases of those who have higher education, the family has two establishments : one, the joint family in the village close to the family property and the other in the taluka or district from where children can easily be sent to a school or college. The husband can also use the house in the district or taluka headquarters for professional practice (in the case of lawyers) as also to keep the social contacts for his political or other ambitions. The wives live mostly in the taluka or district residence with their children. About 25 respondents in the sample have two establishments as described. Some of these respondents limit their visits to the Panchayat Samiti or Zilla Parishad office just on the days of the meetings, when they are also inclined to renew contacts which help their continuity in office.

Economic status of the family

The economic status of the family has been studied through an investigation of the main sources of income, extent of family land-holding and husband's occupation. In rural areas it is hardly possible to expect people to talk about incomes in actual figures. This difficulty is even more real when it comes to interviewing women who in most cases are not quite conversant with family income, property or wealth and who find it hard to make monetary assessments. For answers to such questions they turned to their husband, sons or educated daughter to reply. This reticence also stems from the fact that one is always careful while divulging the real state of one's income or possessions and one may resort to evasive responses. However, the answers collectively given on the three items mentioned, serve to paint a broad picture of the economic status of the husband's household.

Main sources of income

Table 3.5 indicates the main sources of income in the husband's household :

TABLE 3.5 : **Main sources of income**

Source	No. of families
1. Cultivation of family property	117
2. Agricultural labour	2
3. Cottage Industry/Business	11
4. Service Occupation	8
5, Professional practice	6
Total	144

Table 3.5 shows that the overwhelming majority of 117 respondents (81.25% of the sample) depend on cultivation as their main source of income. In Marathwada, 21 out of 22 respondents come from families with cultivation as the main source of income whereas in the other three regions, non-agricultural sources are found to exist with greater frequency. Of the 117 reporting cultivation as the main source, at least 22 reported other additional sources. These range from grocery or grain shops to small mills, some professional practice and even renting house accommodation. It is possible to have a professional practice when one or more members of the joint family take

care of cultivation of the joint family property (thus, with greater dividends) leaving the professionally trained members free to pursue their line of practice. Many of those categorised as cultivators are in fact absentee landlords.

Of the two agricultural labourers, one is a SC woman from Vidarbha and the other a tribal woman from the Bombay Division. The one from Vidarbha did not come to the Samiti office for the interview as the season of transplanting rice seedlings was fully in operation and she could ill afford to sacrifice her day's wages. The local Block Development Officer was considerate enough to arrange for a jeep so that the researcher could be taken close to the field where the woman was working. She came to meet us, sickle in hand, looking rather embarrassed to be seen in her work attire. She agreed to come with us to the nearest Gram Panchayat Office for the interview and was paid the wages she would otherwise have missed. This incident concerns only one respondent but it enables us to see the constraints facing small farmers/agricultural labourers when one expects their participation in community activity.

With regard to other sources of income, the respondents did not have knowledge regarding cottage industries. Business involvement takes place through grocery and cloth-shops, flour-mills, transport transactions. Service occupations are found mainly in Bombay and Pune and these include clerical and technical jobs. Professional practice includes mainly the legal and medical professions.

The next Table 3.6 will enable us to see more accurately the economic status of the cultivators who constitute over 80 per cent of the sample.

Extent of Family holding

TABLE 3.6 : Extent of family holding (husband's family)

No. of acres owned	No. of families
1. No land	6
2. Less than 5 acres	20
3. 5-10 acres	17
4. 10-15 acres	22
5. 15-20 acres	9
6. 20-25 acres	8
7. 25+ acres	62
Total	144

It is clear from the table that the large land owning families are over-represented among the ZP/PS women members. In fact one could even say that the figures may represent lower estimates of land ownership than the real situation because respondents generally tend to claim less landed property than what is actually possessed. Moreover there was no other objective verification of their statements or the acreage quoted. In the actual situation prevailing in the country, the high landowning farmers are a minority in comparison with the large number of small farmers and agricultural labourers who constitute the bulk of the rural population. Again the NSS figures for 1960-61 (p. 3) indicate that the average size of ownership holdings in Maharashtra is 9.42 and 8.83 acres in the 16th and 17th rounds respectively. The present study shows that 70 per cent of families of respondents own land much above the average mentioned. This is a clear indication that the panchayat system is dominated by the category of big farmers. One wonders in this situation what chance land reform policies have where the small farmer or landless labourer is the beneficiary.

The groupings in Table 3.6 on land holding, may be combined in the following manner for further clarity in analysis :

Low	(L) inclusive of 1, 2	(below 5 acres)
Middle	(M) inclusive of 3, 4, 5	(5-20 acres)
High	(H) inclusive of 6, 7	(20 acres and above)

A region-wise distribution enables us to have a more detailed view of the land-holdings of families of women members of ZP/PS bodies in the State :

TABLE 3.7 : Region-wise distribution of land-holding (husband's family)

Region		Extent of land holdings (in acres)			
		L 0-5	M 5-20	H 20+	Regionwise Totals
1. Vidarbha	%	7.40	24.07	68.53	100
	No. of families	4	13	37	54

TABLE 3.7—*contd.*

Region		L 0-5	M 5-20	H 20 +	Regionwise Totals
2. Marathwada	%	9.09	27.27	63.64	100
	No. of families	2	6	14	22
3. Pune Division	%	31.42	48.58	20.00	100
	No. of families	11	17	7	35
4. Bombay Division	%	27.28	36.36	36.36	100
	No. of families	9	12	12	33
Total	%	18.05	33.33	48.62	100
	No. of families	26	48	70	144

Table 3.7 shows that nearly 49 per cent of the respondents come from the High land-owning families, the majority of which are found in Vidarbha and Marathwada ; 33 per cent of them come from the Middle group of which the Pune and Bombay Divisions have higher percentages; 26 per cent fall in the Low land-holding group for which again the percentages are much higher in the Pune-Bombay or Western Region.

It has to be recognised, however, that the mere size of land-holdings does not by itself indicate the economic standing of a family. It is also necessary to know other factors like quality of land, availability of facilities for irrigation more details of non-agricultural sources of income. The researcher found it difficult to probe these areas of information with the respondents and preferred to take whatever observations were possible. Most respondents come from families whose main source of income is land-holdings and the acreage for the majority is high, which represents economic sufficiency if not affluence.

It is of interest to see how far the pattern of land-holdings is related to the prevailing caste-structure in the sample by the following cross-tabulation in Table 3.8. The different castes are grouped as follows :

No. 1—Brahmins and Maratha Kshatriya
No. 2—Kunbis and other Intermediate Castes
No. 3—Backward Castes
No. 4—SC/ST

TABLE 3.8 : **Cross- tabulation of caste and land-holdings**

Caste \ Land-Holding	H	M	L	T
1	46	15	10	71
2	26	9	5	40
3	6	8	6	20
4	1	7	5	13
Total	79	39	26	144

χ^2 Vaule=21.34 ; d.f. 6
$P < .01$
$\gamma = .39$

In the above table the χ^2 as well as the gamma value (.39) show that there is a significant, positive relationship between caste and landholdings. These factors still continue to form a basis for power in rural areas. The traditional combination of caste and economic superiority seems to determine the family backgrounds of the majority of PS/ZP members. The rural poor consist predominantly of agricultural labour households and small landholders with cultivated holdings of less than 5 acres and particularly less than 2.5 acres (Dandekar, Rath ; 1971 : 16). These classes have a comparatively low representation in the sample of ZP/PS women-members.

Husband's main occupation

As already seen in the case of the respondents fathers' the occupation of the head of the household helps to further identify the socioeconomic status of the family.

TABLE 3.9 : **Main occupation of husbands and fathers**

Occupation	No. of husbands	No. of Fathers
1. Cultivation of family Property	96	96
2. Service occupation	17	23
3. Business/cottage industries	13	14
4. Professional practice	17	11
5. Not applicable	1	0
Total	144	144

Table 3.9 lists the main occupation of the fathers of the respondents alongside that of the husbands merely for comparison sake. It would appear that there is no significant change in the economic status of the respondents from the parents to the husband's home. There are identical numbers of cultivators on both sides, which shows that in villages women are generally given in marriage to the same social class of people. The other aspect of note is that some respondents claim the status of cultivator but they take up other activities also as additional sources of income. This side-income in 23 cases even exceeds the proceeds of cultivation. In a particular case the researcher noticed a bidi manufacture undertaken on a large scale, which gave the family access to modern amenities in a rather underdeveloped taluka of the district. Cultivators in the sugarcane belt of south-western Maharashtra, have switched over to other cash-crops and have thereby acquired better economic status. Their additional occupations are proprietorship of shops (grain, cloth, grocery) mills or factories, professional practice on a part or full-time basis and service occupations. Thus one observes a burgeoning of other varied sources of income in addition to cultivation. Forty-seven families, constituting 33 per cent of the sample, have non-agricultural sources of income. Of these 47, Vidarbha has 15, Marathwada 4 and 28 are found in the Western (Bombay-Pune) Region. A closer view of the information reveals that non-agricultural occupation means additional income for the high land-owning sections in the Vidarbha-Marathwada region. The low land-holders are few and many of them belong to backward castes or SC/ST groups. The western Region shows that most of those who have non-agricultural sources of income are low land-holders of mixed castes and their main involvement is with commercial activity as well as service occupation.

One may observe that the traditionally powerful families continue to remain so through professional occupation and business, in the Marathwada-Vidarbha region, whereas there is more of a middle class element in the families having non-agricultural sources of income in the western Region. The increase in the numbers engaged in professional practice is marked. Those in the legal profession are usually more active in the political field and with the increased red-tapism of bureaucratic structures, the dependence of the illiterate masses is increased on the educated elite whose knowledge means more power and a higher social position. The feudal landlords of yore are giving way to professionals of today.

Husband's education

This item helps to throw light on the educational level of the husbands of the respondents, a factor which influences the thought, social aspirations and performance of family members, especially the wife.

TABLE 3.10 : **Educational level of husbands**

Educational Level	No. of Husbands	Per cent
1. Illiterate	10	7.00
2. Primary	21	14.31
3. Middle	39	27.00
4. Secondary	46	32.00
5. Graduate	10	7.00
6. Post graduates/Prof. degree	13	9.00
7. Don't know	4	3.00
8. Not applicable	1	0.69
Total	144	100.00

Table 3.10 shows that the literacy rate is 93 per cent as compared with the male literacy rate of Census 1981 which is 40.62 for rural areas. The largest single group has reached the stage of secondary education whereas in the case of fathers of the respondents the literacy rate was 76 per cent and the majority group was at the primary level. Among the husbands there are more post-graduates than graduates. The Marathwada region stands out by having the highest number of husbands who are illiterate and at the same time the highest number of post-graduates. Graduates and post-graduates are located mostly in the Vidarbha and Marathwadas regions, which are usually stated to be not so progressive. It is also of interest to observe that the high land owning classes belong mainly to these regions. The concept of dominant group seems to expand by yet another dimension, that of education. Anil Bhatt (1976 : 306) remark that the factors which help a caste group to become dominant are numerical preponderance, economic power, ritual status or a high level of education or occupation. Apart from the aspect of prestige and business acumen that education at higher levels induces, another advantage which follows is that educated husbands want educated

wives and in several cases it is the husband's encouragement that has helped respondents to pursue their education at higher levels. Having recorded the educational levels of the fathers of the respondents as well as that of their husbands, it is of interest to cross-tabulate the two educational levels with a view to establishing the educational status of the respondent's family. It is recognised that the influence of father and husband is important in the lives of women. The educational levels have been ranked as follows :

Item No.	Level	Std.	Rank
1, 2	Illiterate, primary	IV	Low
3, 4	Middle, secondary	VII-X	Middle
5+	Above SSC	—	High

TABLE 3.11 : **Cross tabulation of educational levels of fathers and husbands of respondents**

Father's Education \ Husband's Education	H	M	L	Total
H	4	4	0	8
M	11	38	6	55
L	8	42	30	80
Total	23	84	36	143

χ^2 value = 24.58 ; d.f. = 4

P < .01

It is not surprising to note a statistically significant relationship between father's and husband's education because an educated father would naturally want an educated husband for his daughter.

The educational status of the family of the respondent is assessed by a combination of cells in Table 3.11, which permits a classification of the 2 factors into one : Family Educational Background of the respondent. It is important to know the educational status of the family of the respondent to see whether this factor influences the respondent's present participation. Table 3.12 combines the educational levels of fathers and husbands in the following manner :

TABLE 3.12 : **Educational background of families of respondents**

Educational Background	Combination of Cells Table 3.17		No. of Respondents	Total	%
(a) High	H	H	4	19	13
	H	M	4		
	M	H	11		
(b) Medium	M	M	38		
	L	H	8	47	33
	Unmarried Respondent		1		
(c) Low	M	L	6		
	L	M	42	78	54
	L	L	40		
	Total			144	100

Table 3.12 shows that the majority of respondents belong to families having a low educational background. An interesting question that arises is : What is the caste and land-holding status of these 3 categories of educational background ? Table 3.13 will help to analyse the above question by a 3-way table using the particular classification of family educational status as the constant variable :

TABLE 3.13 : **Family educational status, caste and land holding**

(1) High educational status of family (19 respondents)

Caste \ Land Holding	H	M	L	T
1	10	1	1	12
2	3	1	0	4
3	1	1	1	3
4	0	0	0	0
Total	14	3	?	19

TABLE 3.13—*contd.*

(2) Medium educational status of family (47 respondents)

Caste \ Land Holding	H	M	L	T
1	16	6	6	28
2	7	2	2	11
3	0	3	2	5
4	0	2	1	3
Total	23	13	11	47

(3) Low Educational status of family (78 respondents)

Caste \ Land Holding	H	M	L	T
1	18	9	4	31
2	16	6	3	25
3	5	4	3	12
4	1	5	4	10
Total	40	24	14	78

Table 3.13 shows that the cell 1H has the highest frequencies in all the 3 tables. Cells 2H and 1M also contain the second and third highest frequencies in all the 3 tables. This would mean that a high and medium educational background is found largely among the higher castes and large landowners. There is a sprinkling of Backward classes in the 'High' educational background group and total absence of the SC/ST group. There is a noticeable increase in their numbers only at the Low Educational Level. Higher education thus appears as a possibility mainly among the higher caste and high land-owning group. This observation could lead one to say that education and the economic situation of families are closely interlinked. Yet, in the third cross tabulation of respondents belonging to families with low educational status, the largest group comes from high caste and high land-owning families. This would imply that low educational status is not absolutely linked with a low economic situation. Traditional cultural norms still go a long way in determining the pursuit of education in families. The Census of 1951 (p. 144) remarks that the agricultural classes had relatively few who had progressed beyond simple literacy. The three tables show emergent trends in educational patterns among different strata of caste-groups. The agricultural castes which were traditionally low in education, are now

able to climb higher levels faster than others because of their social and economic sufficiency. The backward classes and SC/ST groups are gradually reaching higher levels of education but their progress appears to be limited on the one hand by the process of "Sanskritization" and on the other, economic insufficiency. M.N. Srinivas (1976 : 26) sees "sanskritization" as a process by which a low caste, tribe or other group takes over the customs, social practices, beliefs, ideology of a high caste. This usually takes place when there is improvement in the economic or political position of the group concerned. For instance, in the third part of Table 3.13, row No. 3 of backward castes shows that 5 of them are high landowners, yet they fall in the category of low educational status. At the same time, the greater number of backward castes and SC/ST groups fall in the categories of 'middle' and 'low' landowners and have a proportionate medium and low educational status.

It is furthermore of interest to see how far caste and land holdings may influence specifically the educational attainments of the husbands of the respondents. Tables 3.14 and 3.15 permit an analysis of possible relationships between the variables mentioned :

TABLE 3.14 : **Caste and husband's education**

Caste \ Husband's Education	H	M	L	T
1	15	43	13	71
2	5	24	10	39*
3	3	12	5	20
4	0	7	6	13
Total	23	86	34	143

*One respondent unmarried.

$$\chi^2 \text{ Value} = 7.28; \text{d.f.} = 6$$
$$P > .05$$
$$\gamma = .28$$

The results of the above cross-tabulation show that caste is not significantly related to the educational pattern of husbands. The gamma result of .28 shows a positive correlation, though not at a high level.

TABLE 3.15 : **Husband's land-holdings and husband's education**

Land Holdings \ Husband's Education	H	M	L	T
H	19	44	16	79
M	3	24	12	39
L	1	18	6	25
Total	23	86	34	143

χ^2 Value = 9.16
d.f. = 4
$P > .05$
$\gamma = .29$

The χ^2 test shows that there is no significant relationship between the variables of landholdings and husband's education. The γ test shows a positive correlation even though at a low-level between the above variables. The inference from Tables 3.14 and 3.15 is that while caste and landholdings do not have an absolute influence on the husband's education, yet there does exist a positive range of correlation between them.

Engagement of husband's family members in socio-political activity

This item of information will be studied under the same headings as in the Parental Household :

(*i*) Involvement of the families of respondents in socio-political activity.
(*ii*) Relatives engaged in socio-political activity
(*iii*) Organisational participation.

(*i*) The vast majority of 110 members (76%) had one or more members of their families engaged in socio-political activity. Among the 24 per cent who did not have any family members involved there are particular cases of respondents who made an impact on the local population by their own involvement in community welfare work and so have been chosen as women's representatives on these bodies. Several widowed women figure in this group. The presence of this group of active women proves the effectiveness of thc statute in opening the door to any woman who can work for the development of women and the community at large. The opportunity of being a member of a panchayat body can serve as a means of encouraging the growth of leadership among women who have proved their worth in some way. A case in point is that of a woman who pursued her study up to the S.S.C., though it was not so usual among women in her milieu. Her family gave her encouragement and later she started a Mahila Mandal with sewing classes for women. She even tried to have a creche for children. Her success in these activities made the village leaders request her to be on the Gram Panchayat. Gradually she got involved in political work, the Congress Mahila Front, a Discussion Club for women agriculturists and even a Kabbadi Tournament for Women ! She was declared to be the best woman-agriculturist in her taluka. Her courageous stand at Panchayat Samiti meetings won for her the position of Sabhapati. At the same time she carries her baskets of produce to sell in the market. Shc said that with all this involvement, she gave no less priority to her home. Truly, it is an exemplary success story of women's leadership in rural areas—an indication of things than can be.

(*ii*) The next item investigates which family-members on the husband's side are involved in socio-political activity. The data show that the husband's involvement figures most prominently in the case of the majority of respondents. One-fourth of the respondents had at least 2 or 3 family members active in socio-political activity. In the case of widows the influence of the son or brother-in-law matters. The researcher recalls the case of a seventy-year old widow, illiterate, with hardly any awareness of the significance of a Panchayat Samiti or her role there, having been nominated to be the women's representative on the Samiti. Her son was the police patil, an influential man in the village and another of their male relatives was also on the Samiti. Such incidents illustrate that the provision of statutory representation for women may come to be exploited by some for the furtherance of family prestige and influence. Except for two sisters-in-law who also figure on panchayati bodies, it would appear that there is a setback in women's participation in socio-political life as compared with the spirited response of the mothers during the freedom struggle.

(*iii*) Table 3.16 enables us to have a picture of the organisational involvement of family members :

TABLE 3.16 : **Organisational involvement of family-members**

Name of Organisation	No. of Participants	% (n=144 for each item)
1. Panchayat Institutions	86	60
2. Political parties	89	62
3. Welfare activity	38	26
4. Public office	11	8
5. Miscellaneous	7	5

The number of participants seems rather high because some members belong to several organisations. The numbers in Panchayat Institutions and Political Parties account for the greatest number of participants because it appears that members of PS/ZP are mostly drawn from political parties. Very often the Panchayat Samiti Meeting is preceded by meeting of the members of dominant political groups. Many respondents said that they had to attend these meetings and their anxiety betrayed the impression that they were expected to do so, as representatives of their husband's political party.

Among Panchayat Institutions, most of the husbands are involved at the Gram Panchayat level itself. In Vidarbha and the Pune Division 50 per cent of those in the Gram Panchayats are Sarpanchas, whereas in the Bombay Division, the percentage is 75. In Marathwada, the involvement at the Gram Panchayat level is less; there are 5 husbands who hold or have earlier held office at PS and ZP levels.

Political involvement connotes the influence of State-level dignitaries, Government officials and functionaries of political parties. Till the previous ZP/PS elections around 1973, the vast majority of members and office-bearers belonged to the Congress. Data collection in 1978 happened to be an opportune time, it being on the threshold of another ZP/PS/GP election, when the Congress was divided and had to take a place among other political parties. The respondents were hesitant to reply when the conversation veered round to the choice among different parties. There appeared to be a sense of confusion and disillusionment about leaders projected by the political groupings. An awareness to speak discreetly in terms of ethics used and service rendered was evident. In informal discussions before or after the interview, when members of the Gram Panchayat or neighbours would collect to have a glimpse of the "bai from Bombay", the researcher was asked to help their decision about which party was worthy of choice in the present set-up.

The item marked 'Public Office' includes positions like that of Honorary Magistrate/Municipal Councillor. The welfare field includes a variety of organisations like co-operatives to give agricultural aid to farmers, to better organise purchase and sale of agricultural produce, dairy development as also management of educational institutions, and youth activities. While political manoeuvring gets priority, welfare activity remains on a low key. This is so because a position of influence in Panchayat bodies is more often than not a prelude to gaining important positions on welfare and financial bodies. The husband of one of the respondents, as ZP Councillor also held the position of Manager of an Educational Society, a public Spinning unit, the local KhadiGramodyog Society and retained his appointment as the District Scout Officer ; another an Ex-MLA, held the position of ZP Councillor, and was also Director of the local Janata Bank, the local Land Development Bank, besides being an Honorary Magistrate.

Measurement of political influence in the families of respondents

The foregoing data and analysis on the socio-political involvement in the husband's family permits of broad generalisations which can indicate the level of political influence in the family. It has been seen (Table 3.16) that the involvement of family-members is mainly political while motivation for social service is secondary, even incidental. Therefore, the fact of belonging to or holding position in various types of social organisations becomes an indicator of political influence. The political influence of the family has been assessed on the following criteria :

1. the number of family members belonging to political/co-operative/panchayat/welfare organisations, and
2. the positions held by family members in these organisations.

Each of the above criteria was marked by giving a score of one point for each family-member who was involved in an organisation and a point for each position held in an organisation. The total scores on the above 2 criteria were then categorised on the following basis :

Score	*Category*
0, 1	Low
2	Medium
3+	High

Table 3.17 shows the frequencies in each category.

TABLE 3.17 : **Political influence of respondents' families**

Political Influence	No. of Respondents	%
1. High	92	64
2. Medium	30	21
3. Low	22	15
Total	144	100

The above Table 3.17 shows that 92 respondents (64% of the sample) belong to families having 'High' level political influences. They are mostly in Vidarbha and the Bombay Division. Those having 'Low' level of political influence are few in comparison, yet it is encouraging to note that this group includes respondents who have emerged more on the merit of their own contribution in the community, rather than on the criteria of ascription.

Having assessed broadly the levels of political influence in the families of respondents, it is possible at this point, to see its relevance to caste, land-holding and husband's education. The χ^2 test of significance and gamma tests of correlation will be used in each of the three tables 3.18, 3.19 and 3.20.

TABLE 3.18 : **Caste and political influence**

Caste \ Political influence	H	M	L	T
1	51	8	12	71
2	27	9	4	40
3	10	7	3	20
4	4	6	3	13
Total	92	30	22	144

$$\chi^2 \text{ Value} = 14.08 \quad d.f.=6$$
$$P<.05$$
$$\gamma=.26$$

The results of the χ^2 and γ tests indicate the existence of a positively significant co-relation between caste and political influence.

One may generalise, therefore, that women-members of panchayat who are drawn from high castes also belong to families with a high level of political influence.

TABLE 3.19 : **Land-holdings and political influence**

Land Holding \ Political Influence	H	M	L	T
H	60	12	7	79
M	18	12	9	39
L	14	6	6	26
Total	92	30	22	144

χ^2 value=11.96 d.f.=4

P<.05

γ=.38

Table 3.19 and the statistical tests indicate that there is a positively significant correlation between land holdings and political influence. One may, therefore, say that high landowning families tend to wield more political influence. Since caste is seen (Table 3.18) to be positively related with high landownings one may safely conclude that political influence is exercised in a greater measure by high caste and high landowning families.

Table 3.20 cross-tabulates husband's education and political influence :

TABLE 3.20 : **Husband's education and political influence**

Husband's Education \ Political Influence	H	M	L	T
H	22	1	0	23
M	55	20	11	86
L	14	9	11	34
Total	91	30	22	143

χ^2 Value=20.4 ; d.f.=4
$P<.01$
$\gamma=.60$

The statistical tests show that there is a very positive relationship between the husband's level of education and political influence. The gamma test reveals that there is a higher interdependence between husband's education and political influence (.60) than there is between political influence and the factors of caste (.26) and landholding (.38).

To further highlight the role of caste, landholdings and husband's education on political influence, it may be useful to view these background factors against each group of high, medium and low political influence :

TABLE 3.21 : Political influence in relation to caste, land holdings and husband's education

Political Influence	Section I			Section II			Section III		
	High (92)			Medium (30)			Low (22)		
	Caste	Land Hldg.	Edu.	Caste	Land Hldg.	Edu.	Caste	Land Hldg.	Edu.
High	51	59	22	8	12	1	12	7	0
Medium	27	19	55	9	12	20	4	9	11
Low	14	14	14	13	6	9	6	6	11
	Total : 92 for each column.			Total : 30 for each column.			Total : 22 for each column.		

The Table 3.21 shows that education especially Higher Education plays an important role among the factors connected with political influence. Of the 23 husbands who have had higher education in the sample, 22 are found in the category of 'high' political influence and one at the 'Medium' level but none in Section III. The important numbers of high caste and high landowning families in Section I and II corroborate the findings in Section III. In the categories of medium and low political influence there are families having high caste and landowning status but the differential is marked especially on the educational level. Higher education definitely lends more power to the elbow of economically and socially well-placed individuals in rural society.

What about those of a lower caste status? The data show that among the 14 marked 'Low'-caste in Section I in Table 3.21, 3 have had Higher education, 9 have studied up to the secondary level and 2 up to the primary. With regard to their economic status, 2 are in the high, 7 in the medium and 5 in the low landowning categories. Most of them have additional sources of income through professional practice, business units or service occupation. It would seem that for them the educational factor has been a stepping stone to professional practice, commercial enterprise or the choice of service occupation. Through these activities the economic status of lower caste individuals has risen, hence their greater influence in the socio-political life of the community. Education is thus seen to open greater opportunity to the underprivileged classes for social mobility and influence.

It is interesting to note that among the 14 in the 'low' educational column of Section I in Table 3.21, 12 belong to the 'Higher' and 'Intermediate' Castes and only 2 to 'Low' castes. Among the 12, it is seen that as many as 9 are high landowners and 3 have medium size landholdings. They do not have education but they appear to be fairly affluent which may also count for their selection to panchayat bodies.

From this table it may be seen that education does contribute towards the growth of political influence among individuals in a rural community. In a system where literacy is taken for granted, the illiterate masses are at a disadvantage and look up to the educated minority for help. The disparities arising from caste and economic status may be levelled increasingly if the task of education could be undertaken with greater seriousness so as to allow the more disadvantaged groups to use the facilities available before the gaps between classes are further aggravated by the spread of education mainly among the better placed strata of society.

In the light of the observation that the families of the majority of women-members of ZP/PS enjoy a high status in the areas of caste, land-ownership, education and political influence. What messages are women in these positions likely to relay in terms of welfare or uplift of socially and economically handicapped groups ? To speak of uplift work for the weaker sections naturally means less privileges or material security for the traditionally privileged. How far can women representatives help to generate the movement towards social equality through these panchayat bodies ? One may try to educate them in the area of social concern, nevertheless one cannot expect the impossible to happen. As long as the ethos of a society favours unequal distribution and vested interests, women like others will find it difficult to swim against the current. However, it remains true that the most potent force to initiate the social change desired is in promoting awareness through education.

PERSONAL BACKGROUND OF RESPONDENTS

The third section of this chapter examines the particular sociocultural situation in the life of the individual respondent, which may or may not have helped her to fulfil the role she is called to play through membership in the ZP/PS.

The normal upbringing of a girl in rural areas is directed towards marriage as soon as she reaches maturity. This implies the early takeover of family responsibility. Formerly agricultural households favoured large families and a childless woman was not welcome to her in-laws. Widows too had an unhappy existence and their presence was considered to be burdensome unless they proved to be a managerial asset in the household. Other women in the rural household were counted upon no less to contribute an additional helping hand both at home and at the farm. Their formal education was not considered to be important. Signs of this attitude have been perceived in the earlier analysis of the educational level of the mothers of the respondents.

The rural social scene is now in the process of change. What was something of a dream for the pioneers of the social reform movement of the 19th Century, is becoming more and more of a reality. Education for women is favoured, and trends such as marriages at a more advanced age, smaller families, widow-remarriage are no longer frowned upon. How far does the actual life experience of the respondents reflect this changing social pattern ? At the same time, the probe into the personal background of the respondent also seeks to discover the extent to which the changing social pattern helps women in the social and domestic role they are called to play through membership in the ZP/PS. To investigate the areas mentioned, the following items have been studied :

(a) Age-pattern of respondents
(b) Marital status
(c) Age at marriage
(d) Number of children borne

(e) Educational level and training
(f) Place of education
(g) Comments on education received
(h) Higher education and work-experience.

Age-pattern of respondents

The mean age of respondents is 45 years which indicates the preference for more elderly women as representatives on the ZP/PS. The standard deviation being 10, it is seen that 55 per cent of the sample falls between the age-group of 35 to 55 years. In rural communities, the general norm is to choose as leaders those who are senior in age. They are called village "elder". The oldest respondent was 70 years old. She and others of her age-group had no opportunity of being educated and this became a felt drawback. It was suggested by the women that younger, educated women need be chosen instead of the elderly as in the past.

In spite of the 55 per cent tilt in favour of senior women, it must be recognised, that a fairly sizeable group of younger representatives has also emerged. They are between the ages of 26 and 37, constituting nearly 28 per cent of the sample. Their presence is a sign of change from the traditional attitude which tended to keep younger women a way from the public life of village communities.

Marital status

As earlier observed, the upbringing of girls in rural society is inevitably oriented towards marriage. How far have the respondents been able to adjust to the social situations arising from marriage : widowhood, separation, divorce and what repercussions does marital status have on their membership role in the ZP/PS.

The most significant number of women (113) is in the married group which counts about 78 per cent of the sample. Seven of these had a co-wife status. Not having borne children or having lost them at an early age their husbands contracted another marriage. Among the married respondents widows number 28, and count for 19 per cent of the total sample. Their number is highest in Vidarbha where they compose 24 per cent the regional sample ($n=54$). They belong to a more advanced age-group, 86 per cent of them being of 50 years and above. Castewise, 50 per cent of them are Marathas. As would be expected of women in this age-group most of them have a low educational status. It also corresponds with the low educational status of the respondents in this caste-group. Most of the widows come from families having high political influence. Considering their low level of education, they have imbibed a progressive outlook and even a medium level of participation, which may be accounted for by a greater degree of freedom which they enjoy in the management of their affairs.

When one considers what the position of widows was at the turn of the century it is indeed remarkable that by now their potential as leaders is publicly accepted. Nine of the 28 widows have been nominated as representatives on various ZP. Divorce being against tradition the two respondents whose marriages did not work out have remained separated, having returned to their parental home. They are actively engaged in community welfare work. The only "single" woman in the sample, belongs to the Lingayat community and she works for the cause of education having been a head-mistress of a school for over 30 years.

Age at marriage

Early marriage has been a practice that characterises rural society. It binds the woman to child-bearing and the accruing family responsibility rather early in life. It was of interest to the researcher to see how far the respondents in the sample, have been affected by these traditional norms and whether they constitute a hinderance in their functioning as ZP/PS members.

It is rather surprising to note that over 50 years after the passing of the Sarda Act (1929) which established the minimum age of marriage for girls at 14 years and then at 15 in 1949, a large number of respondents, 32 per cent, have been married below the age of 14 and some in the early years of childhood. The mean age at marriage is 15.62 and taking the range indicated by the standard deviation, (2.59) the vast majority (nearly 83 per cent) come within the range of 13 to 18 years.

A percentage-wise distribution of each regional sample in the below 14 age-group shows 68 in Marathwada, 37 in Vidarbha, 22 in Pune and 12 in Bombay. This pattern of distribution leads one to observe that the agriculturally-dominated regions have a greater tendency towards early marriage than the urban-influenced regions.

Those who are married in the higher age-groups are generally more educated than the average respondent. For instance the 4 graduates married between the ages of 19 and 22 and of the 2 post-graduates one married at 22 and the other at 26 years.

The Committee on the Status of women (1974 : 265) reports that the age of marriage tends to be lower wherever female literacy rates are low.

Number of children

Closely connected with marital status is family responsibility and this increases according to the number of children borne.

Most respondents have families on the larger side, with the number of children ranging between 3 and 5. The largest number fall above the mean thereby indicating that they have had more than 3 children. They are what one may describe as 'experienced mothers'. The researcher noted the quality of experience and maturity that emerged in the exchange of views among most of the respondents as commendable. None of them had read books or done studies on the status of woman, her role, her problems but the views they expressed were in no way 'voice recordings', they were the reflections of women who had lived, observed and sensed the problems of life.

The age-pattern of respondents showed the majority as being above 44 years and minority as below 30 years. Considering that 62 per cent of the sample was married before the age of 16 years, the greater number had crossed well over the child-bearing periods so that by the time they reach 40 or 50 years, their children are grown-up or are already married and settled as would be normal in the rural tradition. Thus one finds that the respondents are largely the mothers of grown-up children and many are mothers-in law which means a position of seniority in the home.

It is interesting to note the number of childless women in the sample : a fairly high percentage of 15. The stigma of childlessness is no longer a deterrent to women's social participation. The statutory representation of women seems to open a door for fruitful contribution on the part of such women.

Linking the three categories of women that emerge in the analysis of marital status, age of marriage, age-pattern and number of children borne, it is seen that the respondents are usually older married women, with a sizeable group of widows and those without children. These three categories of respondents would have a less heavy burden of family and household responsibility. This may be one of the factors for them to serve on the ZP/PS.

Educational level and training of respondents

The educational level and training of respondents will be viewed alongside the educational level of the mothers of respondents so that the process of social change may be more clearly viewed in the lives of women belonging to a particular strata of rural society.

TABLE 3.22 : **Educational level of respondents and their mothers**

Level of education	Number of Respondents No.	%	Mothers No.	%
1. Illiterate	24	16.56	104	72.22
2. Primary	39	27.00	26	18.00
3. Middle	43	30.00	11	7.63
4. Secondary	26	18.00	2	1.46
5. Undergraduate	5	3.44	0	—
6. Graduate	5	3.44	0	—
7. Post-Graduate	2	1.46	1	0.69
Total	144	100.00	144	100.00

The table brings out the spectacular rise in literacy and education among the respondents as compared with their mothers. Whereas 72 per cent of the mothers belonged to the illiterate group, just one generation later one finds that the percentage of illiteracy among their daughters has diminished to 16 per cent.

The largest single group among the respondents is at the middle level of education which would approximate Standard VII. The regional samples show that Marathwada and Vidarbha have their largest single groups at the primary level whereas Bombay and Pune Divisions have their largest groups at the middle level.

As regards higher education, the sample of mothers shows that only one mother was a post-graduate, 2 went up for secondary education and then there is a gap in between. Among the respondents there are 5 undergraduates, 5 graduates and 2 post-graduates. This also shows that the educational gap which was so marked between the fathers and mothers of respondents the ratio of illiteracy being (24 : 72) is gradually narrowing down as evidenced by the percentage of illiterate husbands and wives (6 : 16) in the present sample. Though most recent studies on the status of women tend to decry the low status of women measured among other factors, by low figures of progress in literacy and education, the present study strikes a note of optimism and appreciation at the progressive change observed in the educational level of rural women within the space of a generation. An illiterate PS member aged seventy years had a daughter-in-law who was educated up to Standard IV, a grand-daughter who had passed her SSC and a prospective son-in-law who had a B.Sc. degree in Agriculture.

Eight respondents said that they had taken various courses of professional training, five as teachers, two in homoeopathy and one in nursing. Four of those respondents contracted marriages of their own choice and, therefore, had to depend on their own resources for the support of their families. Two of them worked as teachers and one as a nurse for a short while before and after marriage. One respondent took a teacher's training and worked as a gram sevika. She belonged to the Bhil community and was given the opportunity of educating herself. After marriage, their husbands have gradually acquired good financial situations, hence the respondents stopped working and have involved themselves in social welfare besides political activity as it came their way.

As for the motivation of the respondents, most of those who went for higher education beyond the S.S.C., were motivated to do so by their husbands. Taking up studies after marriage does involve the problem of reconciling responsibilities at home and as a result while some were able to get a degree, others had to stop at various stages remaining at the undergraduate level.

Besides the elite more urbanised group which has gone in for higher education there is also a remarkable group of simple, culturally shielded women who have managed to pursue school-education after marriage. Though they may not have reached high levels of formal education, their record of progress, emerging as it does, through a thicket of conservatism, social prejudice and lonely struggle, opened to the researcher a view of impressive examples of women's leadership in Maharashtra. Here are a few examples :

1. Respondent A had studied up to Std. VII when she was married at the age of 14. After marriage she was encouraged to continue her studies till Std. IX, thus becoming at the age of 16, the most educated woman in her village. The new status regarding the representation of women on Panchayat bodies came into force at the time and as

the most educated woman she was asked to be the first lady-member of a Gram Panchayat. She was very diffident about this sudden plunge into social life but with the constant support of her husband, she gradually built up her confidence to engage in a whole range of activities for the women and youth of the district. She was next invited to be a member of the PS and to attend training camps in other parts of India. She attended an agricultural seminar in Delhi along with two women, agricultural labourers from her taluka.

2. Respondent B, a Maratha Kshatriya was brought up in 'raj-gharana' style, in purdah, illiterate married at 13 years, a widow by the age of 14, with no chance of re-marriage. The utter helplessness of her situation made her resolve to take a little education and in spite of obvious embarrassment in being with much younger children, she studied for two years in the primary section learning just enough to be able to read and write. Today she is an active member of the Gram Panchayat, and the Panchayat Samiti has helped to provide basic amenities (drinking water taps) for the people of her village.
3. Respondent C, now 62 years old, had studied up to Std. IV before marriage. Having had to teach her children she studied with them and managed to pass Std. VII. Her husband encouraged her to study further but his sudden death obliged her to stop her education and attend to family concerns. She took up a job as a teacher in a primary school for girls with a salary of Rs. 30 per month. The school was to be closed because of poor attendance but her good relations with the girls and their parents brought up the attendance and the school was continued. It is thus she came up for nomination on the PS and even on the ZP.

The cases of respondents A, B and C serve to illustrate how education at whatever level, has enabled women to play a more effective social role in rural society.

Place of education

The inclusion of this item is indicated because it throws light on the

milieu in which the respondent grew up, its urban or rural character which may have an impact on the attitude and behaviour of the respondent in her membership role.

The data show that 60 per cent of the sample received their education in the village school, 10 per cent studied in taluka schools and 13 per cent went to city-school. The level of education received by the women tends to rise as one moves out of the village into more urban centres.

Respondents' education and family status

It has already been seen that education is not significantly related to caste and land-holdings whereas it is significantly related to political influence in the case of the husband. It is of interest to see how far these factors may be significantly related to the respondent's level of education. The results of the χ^2 and gamma tests are given in Table 3.23.

TABLE 3.23 : **Wife's education and social status of family**

Independent Variable	Dependent Variable	χ^2 Value	Value γ
1. Caste	Wife's Education	4.62 d.f. 6 P>.05	.22
2. Land-Holdings	,, ,,	7.14 d.f. 4 P>.05	0.7
3. Political Influence	,, ,,	3.93 d.f. 4 P >.05	.27
4. Husband's Education	,, ,,	50.62 d.f. 4 P<.01	.80
5. Father's Education	,, ,,	41.18 d.f. 4 P<.01	.72

The above data point to the absence of a significant relationship between the respondents' educational level and the factors of caste, land-holdings and political influence while indicating a very high relationship with the father's and husband's level of education. The achievement in women's education is less based on traditional in fluence and more on the impact of an educational tradition in the parental family. In the introduction to this chapter, it has been mentioned that it is through the father in childhood and the husband in marriage that the influence for social change is felt by the rural woman. Education is a powerful factor in social change, but the rural woman experiences its effects only after the father and husband have been exposed to its influence. One may say that the progress in literacy and education found among the respondents as compared with their mothers, is due largely to the influence of the educated father and also to the educated husband.

Respondents' comments on education received

The overwhelming majority (93 per cent) of the literate and educated respondents commented favourably on the opportunity they had of being educated. Many regretted that they had not been able to study further because of the social thinking at the time. A tabulation of their comments reads thu[illegible]

TABLE 3.24 : Resp[illegible]nts' comments on education received

Comments	No. of Respondents
1. Can sign my name at least	10
2. Can read and write to some extent	32
3. Able to teach my children	14
4. Can help in family business	2
5. Confidence in social functioning	54
6. Not useful, as there is no time to read, write etc. with family responsibility	8
7. Not applicable	24
Total	144

Comments 1 and 2 were given mainly in the context of the respondents being able to sign their names and to mark their attendance at ZP/PS meetings. The signatures are required in order to avail of the travelling allowance. Reading and writing were mentioned

mainly in the context of being able to read the notice concerning the holding of the ZP/PS meeting and the agenda to be discussed. Most respondents were not able to comment spontaneously on the usefulness of the education they had received, so the researcher had to use certain "probes" and the responses given were mostly an answer to these. Some of the more educated, active respondents replied, "I would never have been able to do what I have, without education". Others said, "At least with a little education, I can follow something, without that, it would have been impossible". Today there is so much paper-work in all these organisations that if one is illiterate, one gets increasingly left out.

Comment 5 has evoked the largest response to include 45 per cent of the literate and educated group. It would appear that to be able to read and write as well as acquire a certain know-how in social life is the major value of the education received. A few of the more educated respondents mentioned the opportunities they had received to develop their aptitudes through singing, sports, and other extra-curricular activity. Education has exposed the respondents to a varied type of group-experience which enables them to have greater security in functioning with groups, even mixed groups.

Comments 3 and 4 show education as having a functional value for the respondents. Comment 6 is a reflection of the wastage that occurs in the educational effort because of cultural norms that do not set much store by the education of women. Many adult women lapse into illiteracy over the years, thus rendering futile the State investment in education and losing the opportunity of self-development by being unable to use the written media of communication. This comment was made by women in 'elite' circles as well as those in less economically favoured groups.

Comment 5 would seem to be the most beneficial one in the development of the rural woman because when one's confidence is built one is more fit to function in society. The traditional protectionism of rural society towards women has resulted in timidity and embarrassment on their part when it comes to playing a social role and taking one's place alongside men in public. It is hoped, however, that the usefulness of education may not be limited to the mechanics of signing or reading minutes. Admittedly to be literate is a channel towards wider social participation but if its main value is reduced to the limited objective of following proceedings or affixing signatures it becomes but another convenient instrument to feather one's own nest. It fails to be a force of social change to improve the quality of life, or to be an awakening of minds and hearts towards a society where justice and brotherhood prevail.

SUMMARY

By way of summarising the findings in the socio-economic background of respondents, it may be useful to compare the dominant caste from which the majority of respondents come with others in the sample on the basis of criteria indicated by M.N. Srinivas. According to him (1955 : 18) numerical, economic and political preponderance as well as a "not too low" position in the local caste hierarchy constitute the elements of a "dominant" caste. Table 3.25 depicts these traits of dominance along with the educational level of the women representatives in the sample.

TABLE 3.25 : A comparative view of the dominant caste and other castes in the sample (Percentage values)

Caste/Caste group	Numer[illegible] Status	Ritual Status	High Land-Owners	Highly Political Influence	High & Medium Level of Education among Respondents
	%		%	%	%
1. Brahmin (n = 12)	8.33	I	58	83	75
2. Marathas (n = 74)	51.28	II	69	72	59
3. Other Intermediate Castes (Agric. + Trading) (n = 40)	17.36	III	56	59	48
4. Backward Castes (n = 20)	20.00	IV	33	48	52
5. SC/ST (n = 13)	9.03	V	8	31	46

The Table 3.25 shows the dominance of the Marathas in terms of numerical and economic status. The Brahmins are dominant in ritual status, political influence and education. The Brahmins in the

sample still retain high political influence but the Marathas are competitors with them. Where there is a fairly high ritual status and high land ownership, dominance is more easily established than in cases of castes having high ritual status without high landownership (Srinivas ; 1976 : 211). Prof. Sirsikar (1970 : 41) points to the domination of leaders of the Maratha caste in Panchayati Raj. According to him it can be stated that the Marathas have numerical strength, economic and political power and ritual status on their side. Table 3.25 above corroborates these findings.

The range of difference in the percentage marking of the different castes included in the table are fairly wide in the areas of numerical, land-holding and political status. The range narrows down considerably in the area of education, especially between the Marathas and other castes, excepting the Brahmins. This would tend to indicate that the educational level of the dominant caste is not markedly superior to others which figure lower in the ritual hierarchy. In spite of having lower land-holdings, and having less political influence, the lower castes/classes have been able to rise on the educational ladder to a sufficient extent as to find representation on panchayat bodies. One may say that the panchayat structure gives opportunity to the educated elite among the backward classes to function on an equal plane with representatives holding traditionally high caste status and influence. Since landownership has tended to go hand in hand with high caste status (Srinivas, 1976 : 211) the backward classes who do not possess much land may never have been able to rise to positions of power and authority in a society dominated by tradition. The panchayat structure thus gives opportunity for a more democratic participation based to a larger extent on achievement rather than ascription.

While participation in the panchayat structure is open to all, education, seems to have become a qualification at the point of entry, helping those who cannot count on traditional sources of status to still find a place and climb the ladder of political influence. It has been seen that the husband's education is an important component of the factors which make for his political influence. The husband's education is very significantly related to the wife's level of education, hence it also has important consequence for social change and social participation among women. Moreover in cases where husbands do not figure, as in the case of widows, even a low standard of education is enough to enable such persons to express their leadership in a dynamic way.

While the foregoing analysis has shown the dominance of traditional symbols of status in the selection of women-representatives on the ZP/PS, it has also highlighted the positive effect of the statute in involving women of varied castes, socio-economic classes, education and personal abilities to make a definite contribution in the rural setting.

4

SOCIAL OUTLOOK AND AWARENESS OF RESPONDENTS

INTRODUCTION

TO understand the manner in which rural women play their role as members on ZP/PS bodies, it is necessary to gain an insight into their pattern of thought and feeling about the social issues that concern them as also the extent of their receptivity and consequent desire to encourage the progressive behaviour envisaged. Any change cannot be effected by mere structural manipulation or legislative action. It has to first find an echo in the hearts and minds of people before it gets adopted.

Since the XIX Century and following political freedom the spotlight has been focussed on women's position in society, the effort being to free her from social slavery often cloaked under the garb of 'religious' and 'traditional' practice and enable her to realise her potential as a free citizen. The Constitution of India has guaranteed the equality of women and successive legislative measures after independence, have spelled it out in different areas of life. However, it has often been said in recent reports on women that the gains of constitutional freedom have not percolated to the masses of women in this vast country. The 'masses' include the 80 per cent of women in rural areas, where problems are said to have remained virtually unchanged (Comm. on Status of Women ; 1974 : Introduction). The system of Panchayati Raj in Maharashtra attempts to provide a structure in which every village, taluka and district has women representatives under the statutory provision and they are expected to play a leadership role in their rural communities (Government of Maharashtra ; 1971 : 148). The progressive social change desired among rural women may be seen as a readiness to recognise the need for change and to shake off their traditional moorings of caste and class to identify with national goals.

It is important, therefore, to probe into the thinking of these statutorily appointed representatives to see what rationale, convictions or attitudes characterise their thought and feeling on the social issues affecting rural women which may also be affecting the whole rural community. The focus of exploration in this study is limited to the awareness of the respondents. Being of an exploratory nature, the study seeks first of all to understand the present thought-content and feeling-tone as highlighted by opinions and attitudes rooted in the social, economic and cultural context of day to day life. Before one applies terms like "backward" or "retrograde" (as has often happened when the telescope is focussed from the urban pinnacle) it is important to understand and appreciate the outlook of the rural woman in her present set-up as obtaining on the village horizon.

The effort in this chapter is to gain insight into the perception of the respondent on the position of women in rural society—the present reality as an acceptance of or deviation from the norms of the past and the expectation for the future. The first part of the chapter consists of a battery of statements which explore the respondents' views on areas of interest and concern to the rural woman ; the views expressed are then categorised according to their tendency towards traditionalism or change ; the third part of the chapter attempts to probe the awareness of respondents on problems and welfare services available to alleviate these problems of rural women. Finally, the emergent trends of thought and resultant action are summarised.

OUTLOOK OF RESPONDENTS ON SPECIFIC AREAS OF SOCIAL CHANGE

By "outlook" is understood the views or reactions of the respondent to particular social issues. The selection of areas of social change was based on the following considerations :

1. Areas in which national policy (in relation to women) has been clearly laid down by the Constitution, legislation or five-year plans e.g. Caste-discrimination, universal compulsory education, age at marriage, dowry, divorce small family norm.
2. Socio-cultural practices in the areas of education, marriage, family and community responsibility, religious practice,

which would reflect a traditionalist or progressive view e.g. co-education, the joint family system, social partici-pation outside the home.

3. Factors of urban influence respondents are likely to have experienced and to which they develop reactions showing their leanings towards or away from traditionalism e.g. being attracted to settle in urban areas, use of media like the radio and cinema.

An extremely important consideration underlying the choice of every area of exploration was that it should be one with the rural women, even if illiterate was sufficiently familiar with to be able to express an opinion. Keeping in mind all the above criteria, the following areas were explored.

(a) caste-consciousness,
(b) urban influence,
(c) education for girls,
(d) marriage,
(e) family responsibility,
(f) social responsibility, and
(g) religious practice.

The statement formulated to explore the above areas, have two possible answers : Agree, Disagree. In the actual interviews with the respondents the statements were worded in the form of questions, since it was not possible for the great majority of respondents to read and mark their own answers. The number of responses agreeing or disagreeing have been noted for each statement. A resume of the qualitative content of the answers given, has also been recorded in order to capture as accurately as possible, the thought-pattern and feeling-tone underlying the agreement or disagreement of views expressed.

Caste-consciousness

1. "Each caste group should have its own services/basic amenities reserved exclusively for them".

Response	%	
Agree	11	
Disagree	88	
Don't know	1	
Total	100	(n=144)

The response shows that 88 per cent of the respondents were against the separate provision of basic amenities of services on a caste basis, some very difinitely so. Most felt strongly about having common facilities like wells for drinking water. A few of the active influential respondents said that they had actively promoted the provision of drinking water facilities for lower class/caste groups since the latter had no possibility of obtaining these facilities on their own. Four respondents, however, felt differently and said, "some people do not observe the up-keep of the common facilities thus making it difficult for others; it is better to have separate arrangements for them, meaning scheduled castes and such others".

2. "Inter-caste marriages should not be encouraged in society".

	%	
(i) Agree	79	
(ii) Disagree	21	
Total	100	(n=100)

The majority of respondents (79 per cent) were not in favour of inter-caste marriages. They did not mind associating with people of other castes in larger social contacts—meetings, social celebrations, but not in the context of a matrimonial alliance. Among those who disagree there are also some who themselves have contracted inter-caste marriages ; a few expressed the view that provided the person was of good character, educated according to their social expectation, they may not resist their children going in for inter-caste marriage.

(3) "Too many privileges/concessions are being given to backward class/SC/ST groups".

	%	
Agree	31	
Disagree	68	
No opinion	1	
Total	100	(n=144)

The majority of respondents (68%) appear to be in favour of concessions reserved for backward class/SC/ST groups. A fairly important number of respondents (31%) opine that there is exaggeration in the reservation of concessions and many an undeserving case may be detected if a follow-up check is done to see whether the goal of special assistance for certain castes is being realised.

Some were reticent to comment on this issue because of the communal furore especially in the wake of riots in Marathwada. The Enquiry Commission was visiting Marathwada at the time the researcher was collecting data there. It may even be that a larger number might have belonged to the "Agree" group if they had felt freer to make their true feelings known. The complaints against the continued giving of privileges were that the practice was being abused by the recipients thus depriving those who were deserving on a merit and need basis. They reported that children belonging to the weaker sections are not being sent to school despite the freeships; they waste time in idle pursuits and do not work hard to compete with others since they know their places are assured. Their parents also do not act responsible, indulging themselves in habits like alcoholism. Another opinion expressed was that the criteria for such concessions be need-based and not caste-based. Financially less fortunate people existed not only among the SC/ST but among other groups as well. In making way for people who hardly stand the test of required qualifications the standard of professional practice is bound to be lowered. When a respondent was casually asked about the renaming of the Marathwada University, she replied : "Today the name will be changed ; tomorrow they will say it is their university and then our children will not have a chance". The better placed respondents specially the majority group of Marathas, generally felt the same way. The researcher was not able to probe the thinking of the scheduled caste groups on the subject since the sample was heavily weighted in favour of the upper caste and more affluent class of respondents.

Urban Influence

(1) "It is better to remain in the village/rural areas, rather than settle in cities".

	%
Agree	92
Disagree	7
Don't know	1
Total	100 (n=144)

The response is clear, that 132 respondents (92%) preferred to remain in the rural set-up in which they had been born and brought up. While for several, this preference may be a projection of a traditional attitude which does not envisage change from the *status quo*, for many others it was a matter of positive interest to stay where they were and do something for the development of their village rather than leave it. Some expressed doubt in being able to usefully adjust in an urban setting. "We must develop our own people here", was the animated answer of most of the respondents. A few who had visited urban areas appreciated short stays there but could not reconcile themselves to a permanent stay in "congested, dirty cities". Many said that there was no question of preference in several cases. There were practical considerations like the necessity of setting with an only son who had opted to make his livelihood and home in the city; or the prospect of a dwindling agricultural economy and the consequent need of educating children for service occupation which could better be done in an urban area. Attraction as such for the so-called glamour of urban life was secondary. A few of the educated respondents who had their education in cities, said that they much preferred continuing agricultural pursuits in their present rural surroundings rather than try to eke out a living in the city. They enjoyed good social status in the village but they had also integrated themselves well into the rural way of life so-as to function creditably as leaders in the local community. Two of them were elected members of their village panchayats instead of being nominated like others.

(2) "There is no need of the radio nor cinema in rural areas".

Response			
Radio	%	Cinema	%
Agree	8	Agree	53
Disagree	90	Disagree	46
Don't know	2	Don't know	1
Total	100 (n=144)	Total	100 (n=144)

It is seen from the responses that most respondents appreciated the value of the radio but felt differently with regard to the cinema. They accepted that the radio brought them news and information which enabled them to learn about other people and problems they might not have known otherwise. "Outside news, broadens our minds" was the response particularly of those who hardly find leisure and are not much used to reading by themselves. For most of them information is passed on by oral communication. Even those among them who had been to school up to the primary level relapsed into illiteracy, having remained out of touch with reading and writing for long. Yet, a couple of them were in good form when criticizing the poor quality of songs and radio-programmes the young spent hours on.

On the whole, the influence of the cinema was not at all favourably viewed. The cinema according to them failed to exercise any useful influence in the lives of young people who are irresistibly attracted to this media of entertainment at whatever cost of time and money. They seem to disapprove of the ideas and impressions projected by the cinema. "The villages were better without the cinema" was their considered comment. Two respondents who had to attend to agricultural work in their own fields, added with a wave of their hands in hearty, rural style : "We have no time to sit and listen to radios or see cinemas, we have to work in our fields". A paraphrase of their thought would well be : "We have no time to indulge in such frivolities as the radio or cinema, because we have to work hard on our fields everyday to make both ends meet".

Some progressive views also came to be expressed in a manner of discussion among the respondents whether or not the radio and cinema could be well managed as a means for non formal education as well as to mobilise villagers' participation in development work.

Education for girls

1. Education for girls is not necessary for a successful life.

	%	
Agree	5	
Disagree	95	
Total	100	(n=144)

The figures above show that 95 per cent of the respondents were in favour of education for girls. While most expressed the desirability of education for girls up to the secondary level, a few respondents did not see the purpose of women going for higher education beyond S.S.C. They felt it was not necessary to expose girls to the experience of going to college for higher education especially if the girl is to finally settle down to rural life with agricultural involvement. What purpose would it serve to let her have university education which may proved to be more problematic than helpful in settling down to life in the village. Moreover, she would desire to marry someone more educated than her and this may not always be an easy proposition. The educated respondents who happen to be also the more affluent) were in favour of higher education.

2. Co-education causes more problems for our society.

	%	
Agree	51	
Disagree	49	
Total	100	(n=144)

It is interesting to note that the group is almost evenly divided on the subject. In general, there is a cautious attitude towards grown-up girls, a reluctance to "expose" them in any way to what may jeopardise their future settlement in marriage. Till the primary school level the attitude is liberal as co-education is regarded as a normal feature but not so at the secondary stage when girls are growing physically mature. Some respondents favoured having schools exclusively for girls, and alternatively that women-teachers be appointed to teach them.

Marriage

1. It is best to leave the choice of marriage partners in the hands of parents/senior relatives.

	%	
Agree	89	
Disagree	11	
Total	100	(n=144)

As seen from the figures above, 89 per cent of respondents favoured the intervention of parents or senior members of the family because they credit them with well seasoned experience which the young lack. By and large, the respondents ruled out exercising compulsion for either boy or girl. The ideal approach was that the matter be settled by mutual dialogue and consent.

2. Raising the age of marriage for girls to 18 years will cause problems for parents in rural areas.

	%	
Agree	36	
Disagree	64	
Total	100	(n=144)

Sixty-four per cent of the respondents were in favour of raising the age of marriage for girls but a sizeable group of fifty-two respondents (36%) preferred an earlier age of marriage for girls, between 13 and 16 years. The rationale for the latter is that grown-up girls should not be kept long at the parents home unmarried. Several respondents explained that early marriage is indicated for girls in rural areas whereas a later age of marriage may be suited to urban girls who have opportunity of higher education and other activities there. A grown up village girl who has attuned herself to the rhythm of her natural surroundings has the longing for early fulfilment in her married life. Any postponement on this score by the time she reaches the age of 16 becomes problematic.

The opinions expressed have their roots invariably in socio-economic structures which open or limit opportunities for the development of the person, and determine subsequent choices in life. In other words as long as different cultural and class structures continue as at present, the one and the same norm of social behaviour may not be valid for all. One need not, therefore, attribute whatever failure of the legislative machinery in this regard to the "unenlightened" choice of a "backward" group but to the need of a group to carry out social obligation for the security of its members.

Family responsibility

1. After marriage it is desirable that one continue to remain in the joint family.

	%
Agree	85
Disagree	15
Total	100 (n=144)

The preference of 85 per cent of the respondents is in favour of the joint family. Even though some of them pointed to certain difficulties which make it inconvenient to live in the joint household, yet there was general recognition of its import of status and usefulness as a prestige symbol of family unity. More so would this be true for respondents who had reached an age when their senior status is well recognised and who thereby enjoy a sense of security. For most of them, living in the joint family meant residing in one and the same household, with common cooking and poding together of income mainly from the family property. A few young respondents communicated in a subdued way their preferences to stay away from in-laws.

2. As head of the household, the husband should make most of the decisions concerning the home and family.

	%
Agree	6
Disagree	94
Total	100 (n=144)

As seen above, 90 per cent of the respondent did not see the husband playing a one-man-show type of role in the house; decisions need be made jointly with the wife. Several drew comparisons with the two wheels of a bullock-cart, which can never run smoothly unless both the wheels operate well together. It reflects the respondents' self-confidence and an awareness of their role which claims recognition.

3. Mothers having brone many children have a sense of pride as women.

	%
Agree	3
Disagree	97
Total	100 (n=144)

The figures show that 97 per cent of the respondents in the sample expressed their preference for small families and would insist on the same for their daughter or daughter-in-laws. Some of the respondents said that they had participated actively in family planning camps and in making propaganda for small families among the women of their villages.

4. Since women ought to attend to the home and family, they are not in a position to accept social responsibilities in the community.

	%
Agree	17
Disagree	83
Total	100 (n=144)

Most respondents were of the view that if a woman was really interested, she could find some time to participate in soical activities of the community. A number of respondents, very much in touch with the local setting said that it was necessary to distinguish between women of lower-income and higher income groups. The former are engaged in daily labour on which depends the daily bread. For these women, it is either work or starvation. Hence, for them, to attend Mahila Mandal meetings, cooking demonstration or such like activities is a luxury they can ill afford. For the middle and upper class women who do not have to work for wages outside the home and who have the security of daily subsistence, the possibility of participation in social activities is obviously there to the extent they show personal interest and have the encouragement of family members.

5. Women should take up a job outside the home only if the family is in financial need.

	%
Agree	20
Disagree	78
Don't know	2
Total	100 (n=144)

Most of the respondents (78%) feel that women can take up remunerative jobs if it is of help to her as well as the family. However, the priority is the home and family and only after these are attended to could a woman take up a job. In the case of women from the lower-income groups, working for remuneration is a matter of course and there is no other option before them. Several respondents in referring to the urban situation, felt that women who came from affluent households need not take up remunerative employment which could be left for the needy people to do. These respondents pointed out that when there are too many sources of income for a family and a superfluous accumulation of wealth, it leads to undesirable effects like lavish spending and luxurious living. It was also suggested that educated women from well-to-do families can use their time usefully by engaging in voluntary social service activity.

The Practice of Dowry, Widow-Remarriage, Divorce

(1) "The practice of giving a dowry to girls should be retained"

	%
Agree	10
Disagree	90
Total	100 (n=144)

As the responses show, 90 per cent of respondents are not in favour of retaining the practice of dowry. However, barring a few respondents who claimed that the giving of a dowry had been virtually stopped in their families, the majority said that they felt helpless against the existing custom and rather than be left out with unmarried daughters, they paid whatever was possible to have their daughters well settled. Several respondents pointed out that the worst defaulters were the more educated people who proportion their demand for dowry according to their level of education. One respondent from a fairly influential family had an interesting tale to tell, that her daughter an M.B.B.S. could manage a matrimonial alliance with an M.B B.S. male only after as large a sum of dowry as the equivalence of gaining an M.B.B.S. degree was agreed to be paid.

An older respondent, aged 65, humorously commented on the modern prospective son-in-law : "He only wants a watch, a ring, a gold chain, to be 'suited' and 'booted'. It was not so much caste or education that stood in the way—a good dowry was the answer ! Most respondents were aware of the evils of dowry, but while a few families had made a definite option against accepting it, others shrugged their shoulders helplessly.

(2) It is preferable that widows do not remarry.

	%
Agree	18
Disagree	82
Total	100 (n=144)

It is seen that 82 per cent of respondents have moved away from the Maharatta Kshatriya tradition of debarring widows from remarriage. Those who are opposed to it still are women of the older generation, who are more steeped in tradition as expressed by two respondents : "A woman marries only once in her life". The general opinion was that young widows not having borne children should definitely be helped to marry again. Many expressed sympathy for the lot of this type of widow and blamed society for the difficulties that such women inevitably faced later in life. The remarriage of widows who have children was generally not approved of. While there was marked recognition of the individual right of the person to remarry if she so desired, it was felt that the happiness of the children should be the prime consideration in the future decision, meaning thereby that a widow will find her happiness in that of her children rather than in contracting a new alliance.

(3) The practice of divorce cannot ensure future happiness in society.

	%
Agree	92
Disagree	8
Total	100 (n=144)

It is evident from the figures above that the great majority (92%) of respondents disfavour divorce and regard its increased practice as harmful to society. The traditional view that a woman married only once in life, also does not admit of divorce. Most felt that a woman should make every effort to adjust and prevent the eventuality of a divorce especially giving due consideration to the future of children. If, however, there were genuine cases of harrassment to women in marriage, divorce may be resorted to.

Religious practice

(1) Religious worship and practice are essential for every man.
(2) Social work cannot replace religion.

On both these issues, there was almost unanimous agreement. The inclination towards religious practice found expression even in ordinary situations of day to day life, for instance, while making chappatis, the first bit of dough is burnt in the fire as an offering to God. Most respondents spend at least a few moments of the day in some form of religious worship, be it the reading of a passage from the sacred books, offering of flowers and incense or some ritual performance of puja, at the family altar. Traditionally God-fearing, they set much store by this daily remembrance of God in their lives.

For many active respondents, "samaj seva" was recognised as the service of God but it was an impersonal projection which could not eliminate the need for a specific remembrance of God be it only to utter His name during the day.

It is also interesting to note that the most popular group activity among rural women is the singing of *bhajans* and religious hymns once or twice in a week for long sessions of two hours or so. The celebration of religious festivals is an occasion which brings women in villages to meet together.

TRADITIONAL PROGRESSIVE OUTLOOK OF RESPONDENTS

The above battery of statements to which the respondents reacted, have been given scores which indicate a trend towards traditionalism or progressive thinking. The statements have been so worded that the "Agree" answers generally point to a traditional position whereas the "Disagree" answers point to the acceptance of social change in the areas concerned. Hence respondents who "disagree" may be described as having a more progressive outlook. The total number of statements is 20. The minimum score=20 points (traditional) : the maximum=40 points (progressive). The scores of the respondents may be seen in Table 4.1 :

TABLE 4. 1 : **Distribution of scores on 'outlook'**

Scores	Frequency
20-22	2
23-25	6
26-28	19
29-31	56
32-34	49
35-36	12
	144

Mean Score = 30.75
S.D. = 3.06

The majority of respondents score in the bracket of scores between 27.69 and 33.81. The mean falls almost exactly mid-way between the minimum (20) and maximum (40) scores. Respondents show themselves to be neither very conservative nor very progressive but the scores tend to cluster on the upper score side of the mean which can indicate a tendency towards more progressive thinking.

In spite of the fact that most respondents come from the conservative landowning Maratha community, the trend of thinking among respondents reflects the gradual change that is being effected in the thought and feeling pattern of this social group in rural society.

In order to correlate the social outlook of respondents with other variables like education, age, caste and family educational background, the scores have been grouped as follows :

TABLE 4.2 : **Ranking of groups on social outlook**

Score	Group	No. of Respondent	Percentage
20-28	Low	27	19
29-31	Medium	56	39
32+	High	61	42
	Total	144	100

Having observed that 42 per cent of the sample tends towards more progressive thinking and that the minority of 19 per cent tends to be more conservative, it is of interest to see what factors may possibly influence the level of conservatism of progress in the social thinking and feeling pattern of respondents.

Education and social outlook

TABLE 4.3 : **Education and social outlook**

Education \ Social Outlook	H	M	L	T
H	10	2	0	12
M	35	24	10	69
L	16	30	17	63
T	61	56	27	144

χ^2 value = 18.42; d.f. 4
$P < .01$

Table 4.3 shows that there is a statistically significant relationship between education and the social outlook of respondents.

This leads to the observation that the higher the level of education, the higher the likelihood of a respondent scoring 'high' on outlook. The observation is borne out more by women at the higher levels of education since of the 12 educated respondents there are none in the "low" group, only 2 in the "middle" group and the rest in the "high" group. Of the 63 respondents in the low level of education, it is noteworthy that almost equal numbers are in the high outlook and low outlook groups. This indicates that the educational level is not the only determinant of the conservative or progressive social outlook of respondents.

A close study of the cases of respondents with a low level of education and a progressive outlook show the intervention of other variables in their life-experience. Some of these cases have already been touched upon in the comments on the educational level of respondents in Chapter 3. A few others merit closer attention :

(1) Respondent W, 34 years, an agricultural labourer, illiterate, works closely with her husband, both in the field of agricultural work and in panchayat organisations. She supported him actively in the last Gram Panchayat election and in demanding a recount of votes since

there was a difference of only 2 votes between her husband and his rival. To supplement their meagre resources during the slack agricultural season, she gets busy with making and selling coloured sugar cubes (a favourite with village children) thus earning almost Rs. 7 per day. She was not happy about the way Panchayat Samiti meetings were held, with the Sabhapati often arriving one or two hours later than the scheduled time. She also told the gram sevika who was present during the interview that nobody cared to inform them about Mahila Mandal meetings or to make any special effort to involve them in whatever activities were being carried on. She appeared enterprising and also alert to happenings in the village and least hesitant to point out the lapses or the negligence on the part of Panchayat officials. Such respondents have the making of leadership.

(2) Respondent X, 45 years, a Maratha Kunbi, illiterate, widowed early with no children of her own, learned the alphabets while other children studied at home. Thus she learned to sign her name and also read. Remarriage being out of the question in their community, she gradually took over the management of the household, supervision of agricultural work and also participated in women's activities, which included giving cooking demonstrations under the Applied Nutrition Programme. She belongs to a large family, and one of her brothers is a Block Development Officer in a neighbouring district. This background partly helped her to be on her own and to become aware of her responsibility towards the community.

(3) Respondent Y, 55 years, a Brahmin, who had education up to the primary level, was married in a Brahmin family and her husband held a position in the local Nyaya Panchayat. Her catholic attitude cuts across the narrow approach of caste or class which is well marked out and much appreciated in the local surroundings.

(4) Another example is that of respondent Z, 60 years, a conservative Jain, who was able to study only as far as the primary level. From a very young age, she was involved in her father's activities in the freedom movement which continued even after her marriage to a young freedom fighter. This background breathes into her a balanced spirit of revolt and service that has come to be known and for which she is respected in her present surroundings. A mother of 7 children, she could not take up responsibility outside the home but she set herself the task of social service through the care of her own children, her employees and their children. She taught 8 boys

and girls to read and write, helped them with their education and today all of them are well settled in life, one of the boys even becoming a member of the Gram Panchayat and Nyaya Panchayat of his village.

Such examples reveal that the social outlook of women with a low educational level has been moulded by other influences in these lives, notably, family influence. Sometimes it is the strong influence of the parental home; and sometimes, the encouragement of the husband and in-laws. While it is seen that education does influence in broadening the social outlook of respondents, the process is not necessarily proportionate to the level of education. The observation that respondents with low (primary and below) level of education have views which are as progressive as those which high education implies that formal education is not the only influence on the thought pattern of respondents.

Social outlook and age of respondents

In rural society, it is recognised that seniority in age is an important consideration in the selection of leaders. One generally tends to associate seniority in age with conservatism. The respondents in the sample are generally above the age of 40. Does age influence their outlook? The following cross-tabulation of age and outlook, followed by χ^2 test, enables one to see the significance of the relationship between the independent variable, age and the dependent variable outlook:

TABLE 4.4 : Age and social outlook of respondents

Age \ Social Outlook	H	M	L	T
H	23	22	8	53
M	23	17	11	51
L	15	17	8	40
T	61	56	27	144

$\chi^2 = 1.97$ d.f. 4

$P > .05$

It is evident from the Table 4.4 that social outlook is not affected by the age of respondents.

Caste and social outlook

It is of interest to see whether caste groups manifest a particular thought pattern tending towards conservatism or progress.

TABLE 4.5 : **Caste and social outlook**

Caste \ Social Outlook	H	M	L	T
1	31	24	16	71
2	20	15	5	40
3	5	11	4	20
4	5	6	2	13
T	61	56	27	144

χ^2 value = 5.52 ; d.f. 6

$P > .05$

The χ^2 value shows that there is no significant relationship between caste and social outlook. Since caste represents a more traditional stand and the general trend in social outlook has a leaning towards progressivism, the above test serves to illustrate that newer forces of change are influencing the thought and opinions of women in rural areas, particularly women-representatives on ZP/PS bodies.

Family educational status and social outlook

Since education significantly influences social outlook, the probability is that the educational background of the family would also exercise a significant influence on the social thinking of respondents. Table 4.6 enables one to verify the probability :

TABLE 4.6 : **Family education status and social outlook**

Fam. Ed. St. \ Social Outlook	H	M	L	T
H	13	5	1	19
M	25	15	7	47
L	23	36	19	78
T	61	56	27	144

χ^2 value = 13.34 ; d.f. 4

$P < .01$

The χ^2 value points to a significant level of relationship between the variables : Family educational status and social outlook. This reinforces the view that education tends to generate more progressive thinking among people and thus prepares them for social change. The fact that educational services are being made increasingly accessible to all sectors of the population makes it a powerful instrument of social change among the traditionally influential as well as among the less privileged, newly emerging sectors of society.

AWARENESS—INTRODUCTORY STATEMENT

The term "Awareness" is used here to indicate the extent of information or knowledge about the surrounding social reality. Awareness marks the first step of the process of social change. It precedes all action for change, especially if the change is desired and purposive. Unless one knows the factors that compose the social reality, one cannot envisage a process of social change. Awareness can involve different degrees of knowing from a superficial consciousness to a deeper understanding of the reality. The measure of awareness determines the vigour and the drive to effect the process of social change.

It is thus important that leaders in an organisation committed to social development be aware of the social reality of the environment they live in as only then can they take proper advantage of the authority and resources entrusted to them as formal leaders, by arranging to plan and stimulate the change desired. Lack of awareness on their part cannot but thwart progress.

This applies also to women-representatives on panchayat bodies. If they are to be responsible for social change particularly among women as a weaker section of society, they have to acquire an awareness of the present social conditions that characterise women's lives. Since this is an unexplored area of study, the researcher was unable to fix in advance any norm of awareness against which the women's 'knowing' could be measured. Hence there is no effort to measure awareness quantitatively. In the case of the women in the sample, awareness means "having an idea" of the reality situation. Women representatives on panchayat bodies have been known, as a rule, not to express an opinion on the social and other issues that are raised in the meetings. Does this mean that they have no idea of these issues ? The researcher felt it would be necessary to ask probe questions and from their responses to assess individual awareness—a qualitative assessment.

The researcher wanted to find out what idea (what type of awareness, if at all) women-members of ZP/PS have of social problems and services that are commonly accepted as part and parcel of the rural social reality. These areas have been spelled out as education, health and employment in the study. One more area selected is the respondent's awareness of the backwardness or otherwise that may be prevalent among the women living in the vicinity of the respondents' villages. After all the respondents are representatives of the local community and are expected to know and to represent local needs and interests. An attempt has been made to study the awareness of respondents in the following areas :

(a) Social backwardness among women.
(b) Education for girls.
(c) Health.
(d) Employment.

Social backwardness among women

The respondents occupy a position of responsibility as members of Panchayat bodies. As women called to play a leadership role *vis a vis* the women of the rural community, their own thinking about the developmental level of women in their neighbourhood is important to discern. Rural women are often described as "lagging behind" the general pace of development by people outside the rural community. The researcher felt that it was essential to listen to the description that women who truly belonged to the milieu, could furnish about the developmental level of their fellow-women whom they see, observe and encounter in the ordinary course of their lives.

To help the respondents formulate their answers with relevance to concrete areas, a series of statements was drawn up, based on the following criteria of backwardness among women :

1. Confinement to the home with little or no opportunity of social life outside the home.
2. Excessive dependency on parents, husband, in decision-making.
3. Limited opportunities of education or gaining of skills which make for self-development or economic independence.
4. Confidence to participate in community activities.

The statements formulated are 6 in number. After each statement the numerical response to the 2-pronged answers (agree/disagree) is recorded, followed by a summary of the qualitative content of the answers given.

Statements

(1) Women in your area of residence are confined only to the home and their children.

	%
Agree	69
Disagree	31
Total	100 (n=144)

The figures show that 99 respondents (nearly 69%) agree that this is still true of a large number of women in rural areas. Society does not permit that women move freely outside the home. In Marathwada, agreement with the statement rises to 91 per cent whereas in Vidarbha and the Western Region the agreement ranges between 61 to 68 per cent. This observation fits in with the respondents' views on not permitting grown-up girls to move freely outside the house. In discussions with mukhya sevikas it was pointed out that even for panchayat bodies more senior women are generally selected, not necessarily because of increased ability but because of the cultural pattern to keep young women in-doors.

(2) Parents and elders make dicisions regarding the level of education, age of marriage and life partner for girls.

	%
Agree	61
Disagree	39
Total	100 (n=144)

Though the figures show that the majority of respondents (61 per cent) are in agreement that such a practice still exists, the percentage of disagreement is fairly high—39 per cent—which may indicate an accelerated process of social change in this area. Many said that the tendency to impose decisions is less than before and specially in the matter of education, the consent or aptitude of the child is considered. The tendency to impose arises more often on the subject of marriage.

(3) Women do not have opportunities to pursue higher education or learn other skills which help towards a better performance of their role at home or at work.

	%	
Agree	72	
Disagree	28	
Total	100	(n=144)

As seen from the above figures, the large majority of respondents (72 per cent) agree that opportunity for self-development for rural women is limited. Women who lived close to district headquarters or in urbanised surroundings admitted that there are opportunities for them to develop skills in home craft. Those in interior areas regretted the absence of such opportunity and were keen that something be done to teach women domestic crafts since they have the interest to learn new skills. In some areas, however, these opportunities are meaningful only to the middle class of women, while the labour class gets ignored,

(4) Women lack opportunities of learning a skill, service or trade which would enable them to stand on their feet.

	%	
Agree	85	
Disagree	15	
Total	100	(n=144)

Nearly 85 per cent (122) of the respondents agree that women should have opportunity to learn a skill, service or trade which would enable them to earn a supplementary living. A respondent made a special plea on behalf of middle class women whose cultural pattern did not permit them to take up work outdoors like agricultural labourers but who also needed to bring financial support to the family. They could be taught some remunerative skill which would enable them to work 'respectably' at home and support the family. Women should be helped to be economically independent especially when a family crisis could affect the male bread-winner.

(5) Women remain very dependent on the thinking of their men-folk and are afraid to defer.

	%
Agree	73
Disagree	27
Total	100 (n=144)

The majority of women (73 per cent) agree about the dependence of women on men mainly in the area of extra-domestic participation. For instance, most of the respondents admitted that they are on the Panchayat bodies because of the influence of their husbands or other male members. Recognising that they are not as knowledgeable as their men-folk in matters outside the home, they are keen to follow their advice. In the running of the home, 90 per cent of the respondents said that there was mutual consultation.

(6) Women lack confidence to take a leading part in public life.

	%
Agree	96
Disagree	4
Total	100 (n=144)

The response to this statement is similar to that of the previous statement. The vast majority of respondents (96 per cent) agree that women lack confidence to appear in social organisations, to speak before men, address groups or take a leading part in activities for the community. "No courage" was the general response. This diffidence on the part of women keeps them out of the mainstream of public life and perhaps deprives organisations of a feminine contribution that could enrich the present male point of view in planning.

Estimation of social backwardness of women by respondents

The responses to the statements exploring the awareness of respondents on the problem of social backwardness among women, also imply a perception of higher or lower levels of backwardness among women in their environment. It is interesting to observe the region-wise assessment of backwardness among women. It is proposed to do this by a rating of the answers of respondents as follows:

Agree	1 point
Disagree	2 points

The response 'Agree' means agreement that women have a low level of development (therefore, backward). 'Disagree' means that women have a higher level of development in the area (therefore, progressive). The statements were administered in question-form to the respondents. Since there are a total number of 6 statements, the minimum score is 6 (low degree of development) and the maximum is 12 higher degree of development). Table 4.7 gives a region-wise distribution of the responses. Scores of the values of 6, 7, 8 are rated Low (L) and scores of the values of 9, 10, 11, 12 are rated High (H).

TABLE 4.7 : **Region-wise distribution of respondents' ratings of social development among women**

Region	L Score 6	L Score 7	L Score 8	H Score 9	H Score 10	H Score 11	H Score 12	Total No. of Respondents
1. Vidarbha	16	15	12	5	3	2	1	54
2. Marathwada	13	3	5	1	0	0	0	22
3. Pune Dn.	13	6	7	5	2	2	0	35
4. Bombay Dn.	9	8	6	5	2	2	1	33
Total	61	32	30	16	7	6	2	144

Table 4.7 shows that the larger number of ratings fall in the low section which means that respondents place the majority of

women in their areas, in the less developed or backward groups. The total of columns 6, 7 and 8 (51+32+30=113) shows that 113 respondents, which is 78 per cent of the sample regard women to be socially backward. 31 respondents (Col. 9, 10, 11, 12) or 22 per cent of the sample feel that women do utilise developmental opportunities in their areas and are thereby less backward i.e. progressive. These 31 respondents come from Vidarbha and the Western Region. The Marathwada respondents are nearly all in the 'L' section of the table. There are no marked differences in the 3 other regions. The assessments of the respondents corroborate what is generally stated at ZP offices regarding the development picture of the regions of Maharashtra which places the Western Region first, Vidarbha second and Marathwada third.

Thus most of the women representatives on ZP/PS bodies are aware that women are, in a way, socially backward and that they need opportunity for self-development. A small number of 4 respondents economically better placed and in a more urbanised environment, felt that women had adequate opportunity in their particular areas. However, it was generally felt that opportunities for women's development were more easily available in urban areas and that these become progressively less as one moves into the remote interior of the rural areas. The felt-need was for occupations ensuring additional income, which while meeting an economic need would also serve to inspire a progressive attitude of self-confidence and independence. The responses on awareness of social backwardness among women reveal that the respondents have a realistic awareness of the situation concerning women.

Education

This sub-section on education aims to explore the awareness of the respondents on the utilisation of educational services by girls in rural areas. It is known that the progress made in the implementation of the directive principle of the constitution on universal compulsory education is yet to be realised in the country and that one of the main causes of the slow spread of education is the female lag in rural areas. It is of interest to know how the respondents of the rural milieu perceive the causes of the problem. Table 4.8 categorises their responses. Some respondents suggested more than one reason, hence the total number of responses exceeds the number of respondents in the sample.

TABLE 4.8 : **Reasons for girls' low utilisation of schools**

	Reasons	No. of Respondents
	People in villages are affected by the following considerations	
1.	Education is not useful for girls	54
2.	Girls have household responsibilities	41
3.	Grown-up girls cannot be sent to schools far from villages of residence	37
4.	Financial problems	9
5.	Lack of girls' schools/women teachers	8
6.	Child Labour	2
7.	Respondents; "No problem in our area"	9

Table 4.8 indicates some of the main reasons perceived by the respondents as blocking the progress of education for girls in rural areas. The highest number of respondents (54) have indicated that education is not seen to be useful for girls. The researcher asked the respondents about how educated girls adjusted to rural life. A few respondents did not see any major problem of adjustment, in fact they said that educated girls made intelligent adjustments in the sense of doing whatever they had to do in a more enlightened way. A few others said that there was no option, she had to adjust to the home and occupation of her husband. Most respondents however felt that educated girls develop a taste for city life and if they have had occasion to stay in a city, they usually do not like to return to the village. If she remains in her rural surroundings, the work that a woman is expected to do—attend to her family, home and field, does not require that she goes to school. Again, even after spending on her education, she finally goes to settle in another home.

One may say that the first-two reasons given in Table 4.8 concerning the usefulness of education for life and attending to household responsibilities are the main blockings among the agricultural labour class of people. Those who have to toil manually in the fields for daily sustenance see the education offered in schools as a luxury which they can ill afford. To a large extent, the first-two reasons are inter-connected. When both parents are obliged to go out and work each day, someone has to look after the house and care for the younger children. One of the respondents belonging to a tribal area in Thana District while holding the view that education for girls is desirable, withdrew her own daughter from school after just one year in the primary section because there was no one at home when she and her husband went out to work. They did not work as agricultural labourers but as they could not afford to hire employees to cultivate their own property, they were obliged to attend daily to their fields. The researcher came across another case in Parbhani District where a respondent having 4 children did not send any of them to school because they had a fair amount of property to be cultivated and they had to do the work themselves. The cultivation of family property with all the economic benefits that accrued was given the priority over education. For this family, education would not increase material production, on the contrary, it would increase the cost of hired labour as well as the cost of educating the children, so its usefulness was discarded.

The third main reason given in Table 4.8, affects the middle and upper classes of rural society who do not like to send their grown-up daughters far from their homes. Nearly all villages have primary and middle schools within the area of the village. High schools are located at more important village-centres or closer to taluka quarters, which means a certain amount of travelling on foot or by bus from and back to the smaller village. After middle-school when girls reach the age of puberty, they are considered to be grown-up, and therefore, not to be unduly exposed in society until they are settled in marriage. Furthermore, transport is a problem in rural areas, specially during the rainy season.

A small minority mentioned financial problems that some needy families faced and for whose relief there was hardly any provision e.g. the Brahmin respondent who could study only up to Standard IV, because of financial problems. A few (8) respondents also spoke in favour of institutions reserved for girls, or women-teachers to teach girls. Nine respondents said that there was no problem in their villages because almost all girls went to school. However, on being further questioned, they admitted that the problem still remains with the poorer, working class of people. The underlying thinking in the reasons given for the slow progress of girls' education is a very protective attitude towards women among middle and upper classes and in the case of the agricultural labour classes or small cultivators, the consideration of economic necessity.

Having tried to assess the awareness of respondents on the problem of girls' education and its causes, the respondents were also asked to go a step further, thus becoming conscious of the social consequences of their awareness. Most of them had to be stimulated by the suggestion of certain options to which they responded. The table below lists the suggestions to which the women responded :

TABLE 4.9 : Suggestions for the promotion of education among girls

Suggestions	No. of Respondents
1. Balwadi/Creche	39
2. High School/Colleges closer to Residence	39
3. Introduction of useful courses specially for girls	32
4. Unable to suggest	31
5. Need of girls' schools/women teachers	7
6. More facilities for poor of all castes/classes	4
7. More facilities for children in tribal areas	3
8. Enforce compulsory utilisation of services	1

Table 4.9 shows by the number of responses that some women made more than one suggestion. The provision of a balwadi or creche responds mainly to those who are prevented from going to school because of having to look after younger brothers or sisters. The balwadi is the most commonly existing service whereas the researcher did not come across the existence of any day-creche. One respondent said she had started one but due to lack of funds, had to close down after a few months. Another educated respondent claimed that she had started one in her village, and that it was still in existence. The problem of balwadis is that there are very few of them as compared with the vast local needs of villages. Further it has been recommended that the posts of gram sevika and mukhya sevika be abolished in Maharashtra (Govt. of Maharashtra ; 1971 : 237) and that they be retained closer to taluka/block headquarters. The result is that these women-workers who were recruited and trained to conduct activities for children and women in villages are now to be found working as clerks in the samiti offices.

An active respondent facing the problem of paucity of panchayat funds, described the following problem faced by the gram sevika in her village : the gram sevika is expected to conduct balwadis and mahila mandals in two villages at a considerable distance one from another. She spends three days of the week in each village and requested that a helper be appointed on a small salary of Rs. 25 to conduct the balwadi on the days she cannot be present. This was necessary to ensure continuity of the programme for the children instead of having to close the balwadi for 3 days. The Gram Panchayat it appears could not afford the amount though the village is a fairly large and important one in the taluka.

Since one of the most important reasons mentioned for parents' unwillingness to sent girls to school was that it was not useful for life, the respondents were asked what courses they would like girls to be taught. The suggestions centered round teaching them courses that would help for the work expected of them : specially home crafts household management, cleanliness, hygiene of the home. Besides home-making skills which are more relevant to the upper strata, they mentioned cottage or home industry which would enable girls to work for economic remuneration.

A sizeable group (31) did not appear to have anything to suggest. It may be partly due to the fact that they had grown up when these accomplishments were considered mere embelishment and not necessary for a woman.

The other suggestions like special schools for girls as well as increased facilities for tribal and needy groups have already been commented upon at various points in the analysis.

With regard to awareness in the area of education the general feeling was strongly in favour of girls' education. About 10 women did not see that the progress of women's education was a problem because in their locality they felt that most girls were definitely being sent to school. Many were aware of the cultural attitude that prevented girls from being sent to school but they see that this is changing. The awareness of the difficulties faced by the under-privileged classes e.g. agricultural labourers is rather low. The respondents tended to answer only from their viewpoint, which is that of the affluent strata. They hardly have any direct experience of the difficulties faced by poorer sections. When probe questions were used especially to draw attention on the problems of weaker sections, the respondents tended to be sympathetic in their answers. Their lack of awareness appears to be less a question of indifference than lack of exposure to such experience. Given the necessary stimulus, the respondents' awareness could be sharpened as a first step towards actual mobilisation of local effort to tackle educational problems among girls in the rural community.

Health services

This sub-section on health services touches on basic amenities that women in rural areas are generally concerned with. The interest in dealing with them is to sense the awareness of the respondent about the services available and their utilisation. The questions covered are : (1) practice regarding confinement and delivery, (2) health education and (3) toilet facilities in rural areas.

(1) Regarding the place which most village women choose to have their deliveries, the vast majority of respondents (114) which is 79 per cent of the sample, agree that deliveries take place at home for the lower income groups and where the PHC is located very far from the village of residence. Usually it is the village dai who attends to the home-deliveries but there is an increasing number of trained nurses and doctors who have set up practice in the rural areas. Where qualified services are available and the delivery is predicted to be normal, women prefer to have it in their own homes. It is only when some complication may be foreseen and the mother's life may be endangered that arrangements are made for hospitalisation. Four respondents made special requests for medical facilities to be closer to the village (present facilities are 6-13 km. away) as in cases of emergency or during the monsoon no quick assistance is possible. Those who lived near block or taluka headquarters where PHC's usually exist, use the services frequently and the PHC's have provision to send their trained medical staff to assist at home-deliveries. Those who use the PHC also tend to be of the affluent classes. Hospitalisation becomes expensive and inconvenient for the poorer sectors. To travel from the remote villages to the PHC or even to a sub-centre, means the expense of transport, someone has to accompany the person, stay with the patient, make arrangements for food all of which cause much expense and inconvenience in a family where adults have to work daily. Respondents would like to have medical facilities close to their village and especially a service to facilitate home-deliveries.

(2) The next question touches on health-education. Table 4.10 given the responses of the women interviewed to the ways in which they may receive some education regarding health. Most women appeared to have little awareness on the subject and so the researcher asked them to relate their own experience in the matter of receiving information on matters of health. The answer reflects the awareness of the respondent about the most effective channel of health education for herself.

TABLE 4.10 : **Channels of health education for rural women**

Channel	No. of Respondents
1. Family Planning Camps/Programmes	20
2. Talks at P.H.C.	14
3. Home visits of Dai/Nurse	69
4. Mahila Shibirs/Mahila Mandals	25
5. Don't know	16
Total	144

The table shows that the largest group of women (69%) know that information regarding health is communicated through the home-visits of the nurse or dai. This appears to be the most effective channel of communication for the education of the rural woman. This also shows the worthwhileness of schemes promoting bare-foot doctors, health visitors or family health workers. Mahila Shibirs and Mahila Mandals also help to impart health education. Several respondents had attended camps run by the Griha Kalyan Kendra sponsored by the State Social Welfare Advisory Board and the comments of the respondents were encouraging about these camps. In the vast area of health, the one subject that most respondents had heard about, was that of family planning. Many had participated actively in the camps organised in or near their village. A few had received awards for their active involvement, drawing other women to collaborate in the programme; one had even given her house for sterilisation operations to be performed during the camp. Regarding talks given at the PHC, the women were hardly able to recall any health education programmes. The facilities offered by the PHC, are mostly availed of in developed centres of the district where the general awareness regarding health needs is higher.

(3) Toilet facilities for women. Respondents were asked whether they favour the construction of toilets for the convenience of women in rural areas or whether such a need does not arise in the present set-up.

A large majority of 91 per cent (132) of the respondents were in favour of having toilet facilities because women are more inconvenienced in the present arrangement. Among those who disagreed, one major objection was that the mere construction of toilet facilities will not solve the problem; women should first be trained to use such facilities, else the problems will be worse than the present situation. As a matter of fact, many respondents said that they did not favour common toilets, they preferred that each house had its own arrangement. Only then would they be maintained hygienically.

In the domain of health as in that of girls' education, the awareness of problems is generally limited as obtaining within the social class to which the respondents belong. The existence of problems and their having to accept the *status quo* is recognised but their thinking on possible solutions did not sound so energised yet.

Employment

Steady employment opportunities for those bracketed as agricultural labour and landless, in rural areas, is a haunting problem. Seasonal sowing and harvesting in the fields, depending on favourable or unfavourable rains, is one traditional opening most of them depend on for their precarious living. Areas with irrigation facilities and the inducement to take to cash-crops, have opened the possibility of more employment opportunities. The official Employment Guarantee Scheme (EGS) has also eased the situation, for both the male and female labour force. It was of interest to the researcher to probe the awareness of the respondents, members of ZP/PS bodies, on this vital problem concerning at least 50 per cent and more of the women in villages. The questions are an attempt to guage the respondents' awareness in the following areas :

(1) Jobs for women outside the agricultural season.
(2) Possibility of a second crop.
(3) Women's wages.

Jobs for women outside the agricultural season

Since work in rural areas moves in a cycle of seasonal employment, it is important to know how women who depend on daily wages are able to find other means of livelihood outside the agricultural season.

The majority of respondents (103) saw the EGS as holding out the most wide spread opportunity of employment for women. Few women were able to use the proper name of the scheme: EGS. They referred to EGS as *bandh-kam*. Ninety four respondents thought that the various agricultural operations, one following the other such as preparation of fields for the next crop, attending to transplanting, weeding, watering till harvest time, keep them well occupied from one season to the other. A smaller number of respondents (18) from the districts of Thana, Kolhapur, Sangli and Sholapur, were aware that quite a few women found employment in sugar, cotton or tile factories located in these districts of the Western Region. Beedi-making a popular industry, adopted by women, particularly of Bhandara District was repeatedly mentioned by the respondents. Eight respondents said that it was difficult for women in their areas to find any employment out of season. Five respondents did not express any opinion on the subject. Four respondents mentioned the exodus of village women towards cities in search of building construction work.

Among the existing options of non-seasonal work, EGS and preparation of soil for the ensuing crop offers scope of employment to the greatest number of women. The awareness shown by the respondents on job opportunities outside the agricultural season corresponds in great measure to the reality situation.

Possibility of a second crop

The first step in agricultural development is aimed at making land as fertile as possible to increase the yield. Since the sample of women respondents belongs to the category of cultivators, hence, involved in the agricultural way of life, it was of interest to explore their present understanding of land-productivity, agricultural inputs, irrigation etc.

TABLE 4.11 : **Possibility of a second crop**

Responses	No. of Respondents
1. Everything depends on the water-supply available	140
2. It is better to have just one cash crop	5
3. The question does not arise in industrialized areas	2
4. Don't know	2

The answers given show that respondents understood the importance of water-supply as the pivot of agricultural development. Ninety-two respondents (64%) said that the water-supply in their areas was inadequate for a second crop. In many cases, even drinking water was not available during the summer months. Several respondents lived in drought-prone areas where the problem of water-scarcity remained unsolved every year. Some respondents who could afford, had their own water-supply through the sinking of wells or hand-pumps. The poorer classes depended mostly on rain or public irrigation works and bore the consequences in case of failure of rains, or the absence of irrigation facilities. The 48 respondents from the West Khandesh area and those settled near the Jayakwadi irrigation project in Marathwada mentioned that they successfully arrange for two field-crops from their lands because of the good irrigation facilities available. Most of the women thus showed awareness of the crucial problem of water-supply in the agricultural economy.

Women's wages

Inequality between wages paid to men and women is regarded as unlawful discrimination on ground of sex and a violation of social justice. National legislation has sought to remedy the situation by condemning such discriminatory action in conformity with the ILO decision (U.N. Convention, 1951 ; Recommend of National Comm. of Labour, 1975, Govt. of India, 1975 : 2, 3). "Equal pay for equal work" has become a slogan in favour of women's emancipation.

The respondents were asked whether men and women in their area were paid equally for work done. In case they answered in the negative, they were asked the reason for this unequal payment.

A majority of 123 respondents (85%) were aware that there is a difference in wages paid to men and women in the rural, agricultural setting. Ninety-seven respondents (67%) feel that the difference is justified in view of the fact that men do heavier jobs than women. A fairly important group of 43 women (30%) do not approve of this practice and feel that its existence brings into focus the traditional injustice meted out to women. Among the group of 43 there were women who were directly in touch with the field and thus had strong conviction on this point. Some of the more protected respondents from affluent families who had little contact with the field merely repeated the answers suggested by others. The problems of labour, payment of wages touched them rarely because they were less involved in the management of family property. Besides, the socially higher class of respondents keeps a distance from the agricultural labour class except when they provide the afternoon meal to workers. Many respondents had just accepted the situation as it has always existed. When the researcher asked a particular respondent whether she thought it all right that women be paid less wages for work equal to that done by men, she replied that she had not thought of this before. On discussing the issue she definitely felt that the practice was not justified. A few minutes later, when her husband, who had returned from the supervision of work in the fields, was being served his noon meal, she commented to him that it was not fair that women be paid less wages than men. He animatedly defended the existing situation, giving a string of reasons why women cannot justify this claim. Not being in the know of these matters, she was not in a position to reply, but the debate had been opened—she was ready to find out more about the question !

SUMMARY

The main findings of the analysis on the social outlook and awareness of respondents may be summarised as follows :

1. The respondents show themselves to be fairly progressive in outlook, ready to recognise the demands of a changing social situation, whether in the demand of education, marital rights or socio-economic participation. Even in cases when some adopt a more traditional stance as on the issue of the age of marriage, their approach is guided by practical reasoning in the existing circumstances rather than by any rigid holding to the past. They thus show themselves to be amenable to whatever change is found to be desirable in the light of the new social context.

2. Education is seen to be a significant factor in the more progressive outlook of woman specially among those with higher education. At the same time there are examples to illustrate that respondents with a low level of education have a progressive approach to the various situations envisaged, which only shows that formal education is not the sole factor in shaping the social interests and attitudes of rural women.

3. The investigation on the respondents' awareness of social backwardness among women reveals their own assessment that both the poorer classes who are preoccupied with earning the daily bread as well as the affluent among them, tend to remain isolated from the mainstream of public life. In this context, one may say that the statutory representation of women does help to break the process of alienation of women from public life by making their presence on Panchayat bodies obligatory. Yet it is not the mere fact of being physically represented that is enough. Representation must gradually

open the way to participation in the work of the panchayat body as the barriers in the socio-economic fabric of rural society get eliminated and the personal ability of women finds confident expression.

4. Social legislation has to reconcile with the socio-economic structure of the rural community. The freedom guaranteed by present social legislation in favour of women cannot but be related to women's ability to achieve a certain measure of independence as a person in society. For instance, without the opportunity of education or the possibility of being economically independent, one cannot expect to postpone the age of marriage indefinitely in a society which has always regarded marriage as the necessary fulfilment of a woman's life. The answers of the respondents show their awareness of the link between the observance of social legislation and the general developmental level of society.

5. The opinions expressed on marriage and family life reveal a deep-seated respect for the sacredness of the marriage bond and duties towards members of the family. On the one hand there is the traditional regard for the husband's position in the home but there is also an awareness of their own position as co-partners having an equal share in the conduct of domestic affairs. The institution of marriage involves compelling duties and obligations of family life which are not to be sacrificed for social participation more so on the part of women.

6. Statutory representation for women, therefore, is a challenge for the family of the respondent because the woman's involvement in community work automatically calls for adjustments on the domestic scene. The data also showed that women in general take up membership in ZP/PS bodies beyond the age of 40 years or so when the burden of family responsibility is comparatively reduced and they can move outside the home with greater freedom. Above all the encouragement and cooperation of family members go a long way towards helping women to participate in community programmes. An interesting case came up where a respondent educated up to the primary level, whose husband had not gone to school, preferred to avoid the lime-light of social participation lest her husband feel any embarrassment.

7. On widow re-marriage, most respondents held that if she had children by her first marriage their happiness should be her first consideration. In the case of young widows without children, it is desirable that they re-marry.

In view of the encouraging response received from the respondents. The author cannot help mentioning that whenever she contacted official agencies in order to find the whereabouts of women representatives on ZP/PS bodies and asked for some preliminary information about them, the usual implied reaction was "We do not know much about her. Anyway, what will she tell you ? She never opens her mouth at meetings". Even gram sevikas and mukhya sevikas discouraged the researcher from travelling all the way to the residence of many a respondent saying that not much may be gained by interviewing her. However, at the end of a few interviews more than one mukhya sevika exclaimed, "I really never thought that this woman would be able to express herself so well to you". The statute has helped to lay the foundation for eliciting women's participation in the mainstream of social life.

However, laying the foundation is not enough. One has to believe in the potential that women-representatives have and know how to tap their strengths. If not, things may happen like in a Vanjara village where a local MLA wanted to show great esteem for women in having an all women's panchayat for the village. The women were thrust into positions they were totally unprepared for. At the same time, they had to attend to all domestic chores as usual including services to their more idle husbands, and the men looked on, their tongues in their cheeks, ready to conclude : "You saw, even when we elected them they could not do anything."

In the measure that women help each other to make the best of this opportunity to effect growth in themselves and perceive the social situation around them, in that measure will they be stimulated to think creatively and act effectively. The challenge has been accepted and the process can be said to have begun.

5

SOCIAL PARTICIPATION OF RESPONDENTS

INTRODUCTION

THE ultimate test of development endeavour is action for development just as the ultimate efficacy of legislative effort lies in its ability to effect the social change as envisaged by its measures. This study has so far described the socio-economic background and social outlook of respondents, members of ZP/PS bodies, but the efficacy of the panchayat statute on women's representation lies in its ability to mobilise the members into developmental action for the rural community. Investigation in the area of their social participation aims at discovering the type of social involvement that characterises women-representatives as members of the ZP/PS and of other social organisation.

The approach is exploratory, not fixing in advance the criteria against which to compare the performance of respondents. Also, there is nothing to go by as the existing studies on women in India hardly cover women in villages and there are none on their participation in village panchayats ; the studies that exist, are for the most part, urban-based. The approach here is to discover and understand the present pattern of functioning and what possibly helps or hinders the respondent in playing her social role as a ZP/PS member.

The exploration into the pattern of social participation is done keeping in mind the traditional norms of rural culture which affect the behaviour of village women as described earlier. As a rule they give themselves fully to the home and children and do not take up any active role in public. Against this background, the statute calling for the presence of one or two women in a male-dominated panchayat meeting can be said to be revolutionary. The questions that naturally arise from this initiation of rural women into public life are: what is the social action resulting from women's representation on these bodies? Given the traditionalism of their social background, how far are they able to launch out into community action as expected? How far does the social milieu create an atmosphere of encouragement for women to actively meet the challenge of social participation as posed by the statute? What do the respondents themselves feel about the new role they are called to play?

These questions have stimulated the quest in this study and have helped to give direction to its exploratory endeavour. Issues such as the exercise of power, influence, decision making, are part of the process of social action and would need to be included in any study which focusses on the social performance of leaders, both men and women in a body such as the ZP/PS. In this particular case, the study focusses on women who are "formal" leaders. Any fixed criteria to assess their social participation as would be possible in the case of men who have always been in the forefront of leadership in the rural community, may be found totally inoperative in the case of rural women. Yet, the implementation of the status for over 20 years in Maharashtra shows that some "stirring to life" has begun among women. Their response has started taking shape. In different regions of the State, the response will have varying shades of involvement and impact, depending on a network of factors which this investigation proposes to explore to the extent possible. Launching into an unexplored area, the study attempts to focus on the present response in actual social conditions, thereby also bringing to light the potential that exists. The rural social context is not static; there is enough data even in the present study to testify to the process of social change to which the milieu is responsive. This study, therefore, implicitly reflects the impact of past or passing social influences, the present style of operation and the trends of future participation among rural women.

A detailed analysis of the respondents' social participation as outlined in the plan, follows :

GENERAL SOCIAL PARTICIPATION OF RESPONDENTS

Under this title it is proposed to present a picture of organisational membership which may help characterise the social experience of the respondents. In studying the organisational experience of respondents, the following questions arise :

(a) What social/political organisations, if any, do the respondents belong to ?
(b) How far are they involved in the programmes of these organisations ?
(c) What opportunities do they have in gaining knowledge and experience so as to improve their membership performance ?

These questions will be investigated under the following heads :

(a) Membership in social organisations.
(b) Extent of participation in organisations.
(c) Participation in camps/training courses.

Membership in social organisations

The fact that a woman belongs to various social organisations and is involved to a greater or lesser extent in various community programmes is one indication of her active social involvement with the community. The organisations which will be mentioned in the following Table 5.1 may not be the only ones existing in rural areas but they are the ones which the respondents are generally concerned with. The respondents were asked to mention which organisations they belonged to before their appointment as ZP/PS members and which ones they joined after their nomination. The following Table 5.1 lists the organisations :

TABLE 5.1 : **Membership of respondents in social organisations**

Organisation	No. of Respondents	
	Before Nomination to PS/ZP	After
1. Panchayat bodies	80	144
2. Mahila Mandals	64	60
3. Family and Child Welfare Committee	11	13
4. District Cooperatives/Banks	11	20
5. Municipality/Welfare Organisations	4	3
6. Political Party	67	92
7. Any other	13	23
8. None	35	26

It is seen from the table above that the majority of members (80) had already had some experience of membership in panchayat bodies. A further analysis of the data gathered shows that 61 respondents had been in Gram Panchayats for varying periods of 5 to 10 years, 34 respondents had already been members of the PS and 14 had been members of the ZP. Again while 42 respondents had the experience of belonging only to the Gram Panchayat (GP), 13 respondents had belonged both to the GP and PS and 5 belonged to all the bodies at the three levels of the Panchayat structure (GP, PS and ZP). Of those who were elected or nominated to the GP, 6 had held the position of sarpanch and 2 that of upasarpanch. Among those in the PS, 3 respondents had occupied the position of upasabhapati for temporary periods. One respondent had the unique honour of being elected to the chairmanship of the Zilla Parishad. The Gram Panchayat has provided grass-root experience for the majority of respondents which is the desired process in the growth of leadership among women in panchayat bodies.

The next important group (67) is involved in local units of political parties. The involvement in political activity increased after the women became members of the ZP/PS.

A third important group of women (64) is that of members of Mahila Mandals. There is a difference of 4 in the numbers before and after nomination to the ZP/PS and that is due to the closure of some Mahila Mandals for one reason or the other. A few respondents have played a pioneering role in starting Mahila Mandals in their villages. Nearly fifty per cent of those active in Mahila Mandals have been or are presidents of their units. Their activities cover socio-religious celebrations like the Sharada Utsav which is specially observed by women, "*Huldi Kumkum*", the singing of *bhajans* besides cutting and sewing classes as well as cooking demonstrations. Some members made commendable effort to conduct balwadis and even adult-education classes. In one case, the Mahila Mandal raised funds for the balwadi of the village. On the other hand, several respondents appeared to be discouraged because their efforts had not met with co-operation from women in the local community. Where there is a gram sevika or mukhya sevika appointed, the activity of Mahila Mandals is more sustained and regular. The Miraj Block was a good illustration of co-operative endeavour among gram sevikas and mukhya sevikas of the ANP and FCW (Family and Child Welfare) programmes. The interest of these workers reveals itself in the vitality of women's participation which appeared to be higher there than in other blocks. When the researcher asked them how they managed to extend the scope of their activities to so many villages when personnel was limited, it was explained how they sought the cooperation of other functionaries such as nurses and teachers to initiate women's activities so that an ever widening circle of women became socially involved. The work of gram sevikas and mukhya sevikas has often gone unseen and unrecognised but much of the development that has taken place among rural women today may be traced to their efforts begun at the grass-roots, encouraging women to unite and make their contribution both inside as well as outside the home. If panchayat bodies could encourage such trained workers to team up with women-members in the area of development activity for local women, it would go a long way in helping the growth of leadership at the village level.

With regard to co-operatives, more women seem to have been appointed on the managing committees of co-operatives concerned with agricultural aid and marketing. These appointments are also politically biased. In order to encourage rural women to put by some savings, the Mahila Bank actively involved 5 respondents who mobilised many women to start savings schemes. Another activity applying specially to women is the Farmers' Discussion Club which encourages women engaged in agricultural work to learn about new methods introduced in agriculture.

Table 5.1 shows that there were 2 respondents in Municipal Councils and 8 respondents were Honorary Magistrates. These were among the more educated respondents who live either in or very close to urban centres. Thirty-five women said that they had not had experience of social participation before becoming members of the ZP/PS. Twenty-six of these continue as mere 'register' members of the ZP/PS with no further social involvement.

The data in Table 5.1 draws attention to the political involvement that colours membership in various rural social organisations and which inevitably affects women-participants. At the same time there are instances of women's initiatives in welfare/development activity for women and children. That such instances of women's intervention should be multiplied as a result of her membership on panchayat bodies is the most desirable outcome. The major challenge of statutory representation for women lies in its ability to use political influence to effect women's development from the village level upwards.

Measurement of organisational membership

In order to be able to assess quantitatively the social participation of women, each quantifiable item will be measured at the end of a qualitative analysis of the pertinent data. With regard to organisational membership, the qualitative analysis having been done, the quantitative assessment follows. The ratings of High, Middle and Low will be based on scores given according to the number of organisations in which the respondent is a member. Those who have never belonged to or do not belong to any organisation other than the actual ZP/PS score 0 points. Those who may have belonged or presently belong to any organisation other than the actual ZP/PS score points according to the number of organisations they may have belonged or presently belong to. The assessment of participation through organisational membership it thus as follows :

TABLE 5.2 : **Organisational membership**

No. of Organisation	Score	Rating	No. of Respondents	
None	0	Low	43	
1	1	Low		
2	2	Middle	39	65
3	3	Middle	26	
4 and above	4+	High	36	
		Total	144	

The above rating of social participation is only a general indicator, not an absolute measure because it indicates a participation that may be extensive without effective involvement of the person of the respondent. For instance there was the case of a respondent who belonged to the PS and ZP of her district but it was her husband who did whatever active work had to be done outside the house. A month after the interview, the researcher met the husband in Bombay, as among other things, he had come to see whether his wife's name could be put on a committee at the State level. For him, this was one way of increasing the range of his own influence. In spite of the above-mentioned limitations it has to be admitted that in the present social set-up, for a woman to belong to various social or political organisations at the village, taluka or district levels, is an indication of her power and social influence—whether its source is in herself or vested in the family.

A region-wise distribution of the scores of respondents in the range of organisations of which they are or have been members reads as follows :

TABLE 5.3 : **Region-wise distribution of scores in organisational membership**

Region	Scores							
	Low 0, 1		Middle 2, 3		High 4+		Total	
		%		%		%		%
1. Vidarbha	18	23	25	46	11	21	54	100
2. Marathwada	5	23	12	54	5	23	22	100
3. Pune Division	10	28	16	46	9	26	35	100
4. Bombay Division	10	30	12	36	11	34	33	100
	43		65		36		144	

The Table 5.3 shows that the great majority of respondents (43+65=108) have a membership range that goes up to 3 organisations. Further break-up of the column marked "Middle" reveals that 39 respondents belong to 2 organisations and 26 to 3 organisations. This means that the majority of respondents (43+39) which accounts for 57 per cent of the sample, fall in the category of those who belong to two organisations and below. Of these, membership of a political party is the most common feature. Among the four regions of the State, the Bombay Division appears to have the most equitable distribution among the 3 levels of participation. It also has the highest percentage of women in the High membership group. The particular districts with the highest concentration of respondents who have wide-ranging membership, are Thane and Nagpur and these respondents operate close to the metropolitan cities of Bombay or Nagpur. The membership range in the sample shows a variation from 0 indicating the presence of respondents who belong only to the ZP/PS (under persuasion) to a score of 10 points indicating the extremely wide range of membership on the part of some respondents. An example of high scoring membership is the following :

Respondent M—Sarpanch for 10 years.
—Elected Councillor and President of the Zilla Parishad

—President of the Taluka Mahila Mandal
—Member of State Social Welfare Advisory Board
—General Secretary of the District Unit of a Political Party
—Member of the Educational Committees of 5 High Schools
—Member of the Governing Council of a College
—Councillor in a University
—Director, District Central Co-operative Bank
—Member, State Land Reclamation and Development.

This example of high ranging membership is enacted against a background of political involvement of the family, education in an urban surrounding and the personal drive of the respondent. Those with high-ranging membership scores in the Thana and Nagpur districts show similar traits of background influence. Respondents living either in or close to urbanised centres tend to have a wider range of membership, partly because of the increased facilities of transport and communication.

Extent of participation in programmes

Under this title it is proposed to examine the extent of involvement that the respondent may have in any one or more of the organisations (excluding ZP/PS) of which she may have been or still is a member. The inclusion of this item helps to give a more correct picture of the actual participation of women by focussing on personal performance rather than relying merely on scores of high-ranging membership which may be more a projection of environmental influences rather than a manifestation of personal ability in social participation. Several respondents were actively engaged in only one or two organisations and their qualitative social participation would not be reflected in the range of organisations in which respondents have membership. The criteria selected to measure extent of programme-participation cover the following areas :

—attendance at meetings
—involvement in continuing programmes
—initiatives taken to start new activities.

Table 5.4 measures the extent of involvement in the programme of the organisations in which respondents claim membership. Each item has been given a score which places the extent of participation in 3 categories : High, Middle, Low. The numbers of respondents in each category is also marked :

TABLE 5.4 : **Extent of involvement in programmes**

Extent of Involvement	Score	Rating	No. of Respondents
1. No involvement	0	Low (L)	3
2. Occasional attendance at meetings	1	Low (L)	23
3. Regular attendance	2	Middle (M)	36
4. Active participation in programmes	3	High (H)	46
5. Initiation of new activities	4	High (H)	36
		Total	144

Table 5.4 shows that the majority of respondents (46+36 =82) are in the high-participation group. The contract with Table 5.2 is striking because most members were in the low-participation group when range of membership was measured.

The criteria selected to indicate extent of participation as seen in Table 5.4 takes into consideration the existing local picture concerning women's involvement in organisations. 'No involvement' means that the respondent does not belong or has not belonged to any organisation other than the ZP/PS of which she is a member. 'Occasional attendance at meetings' means that the respondent limits herself to the minimum attendance required of a member. 'Regular attendance' indicates that the woman attends nearly all the meetings but finds it difficult to involve herself other than marking her attendance at meetings. 'Active participation' indicates that the respondent actively involves herself in programmes undertaken by the organisation. 'Initiation of new activities' denotes a higher level of involvement than active participation in the regular programmes since it indicates the pioneering ability of the respondent to start a programme where none existed before or for reviving one.

Among the respondents who attend meetings occasionally or regularly are to be found several who desire to be further involved because they see that the responsibility of membership entails far more than signing the register of attendance. At the same time they admit that they are not able to give more time to the organisation because of household responsibilities.

Of those who actively participate in programmes, many are actives in political parties and their busiest days are those at the moment of elections. It is then that they make contacts among women, canvassing for votes by paying house to house visits.

Some commendable initiatives which the respondents reported were the starting of Mahila Mandals, bhajan-groups in the homes of respondents, craft classes, adult education among women and welfare activities for children. The continuity of these activities was sometimes rendered difficult by group-conflicts and lack of funds.

The data collected under this item reveals a broad pattern of organisational involvement among rural women. It is heartening to know that a majority of women-members do make efforts to involve themselves actively in the organisations to which they belong. However, the data need to be further studied using more objective sources which could help to reveal the detailed pattern of social involvement among women.

Travel/Supervisory tours

Under this heading, social participation is seen in terms of the amount of travel that membership in an organisation may demand and how far women are able to cope with it. Belonging to an organisation which exists not only at the village level but also at the taluka, district or State levels implies that women widen the sphere of their interest and activity beyond the local circle of the village. To attend meetings outside one's village, to undertake tours of certain areas is an indication of wider social participation. The question on the 'travel' seeks to find out how many respondents have been/are exposed to the experience of travelling or touring outside the village as part of their membership responsibility. Each response is given a score which indicates a higher, middle or lower degree of participation, as seen in Table 5.5.

TABLE 5.5 : **Travel undertaken in organisational membership**

Response	Score	Rating	No. of Respondents
1. Never	0	L	112
2. Rarely	1	M	12
3. Often	2	H	20
Total			144

Table 5.5 shows that 112 respondents (78% of the sample) do not belong to organisations which expose them to the experience of travelling outside the village, or the taluka centre. The 20 respondents who travel often, belong to organisations at the district or State levels which oblige them to travel for meetings or as in the case of the State Social Welfare Advisory Board, to supervise the working of welfare centres established in different parts of the district. With the exception of 3, all the rest of the 20 respondents have either their own residential establishment or that of close relatives in the district headquarters or city in which they have to visit. Staying on for 2 or 3 days, therefore, poses no problem for them.

Women in rural areas do not normally take up work which obliges them to travel for long distances or to make overnight halts. Since transport is not always regular and sufficiently widespread in the districts, there is a limit to the distance one can cover within the space of a day. Already, much improvement in transport and communication has been achieved. Since the State Transport Bus Service has become the main means of transport for members of the ZP/PS. However, the question of women's accommodation and overnight stay does pose a problem. During the monsoon these problems of transport are further aggravated by the inaccessibility of roads. This may be an added reason for women's participation being confined to the local bodies like the Gram Panchayat and the village Mahila Mandal. At the level of political activity too, most respondents usually undertake house to house contacts in the village, for election purposes. Wider contacts at the district and state levels are usually undertaken by respondents with established urban contacts.

A highly educated respondent in Marathwada said that she always took one of her children with her when she toured areas in the district because she felt very awkward to halt at "rest houses" alone. The researcher can corroborate these observations by her own experience while travelling alone through the districts, having had to find accommodation at times in "guest houses" or "rest houses". The arrangements made under Government auspices, in this regard were helpful.

Addressing groups of people

Under this item it is proposed to find out how many respondents have had the experience of encountering people in groups and addressing them. As representatives appointed on the ZP/PS, the respondents are called to play a leadership role vis-a-vis the women of their taluka or district. To address a group implies an ability to communicate and to mobilise groups of people to work together for a specified goal. In this sense, the experience of addressing groups of people constitutes an important channel of social participation. Table 5.6 shows how far respondents have been able to use this tool as means of becoming more involved with the local community. Each response is given a score which indicates a higher, middle or lower level of this particular form of social participation :

TABLE 5.6 : **Experience of addressing people**

Response	Score	Rating	No. of Respondents
1. Never	0	L	71
2. Rarely	1	M	53
3. Often	2	H	20
Total			144

Table 5.6 shows that nearly 50 per cent (71) of the respondents in the sample have never been exposed to speaking to a group of people and could hardly even envisage the possibility of doing so. Those in the group marked "rarely" are respondents who have been called to address school children or groups of women at the Mahila Mandal Meetings once in a way on the occasion of a national festival or a cultural programme. The group marked 'often' consists of almost all the 20 respondents who travel often (Table 5.5). Many of these have stood for general elections to the ZP since they hail from families that are politically active.

The items that have been examined in the foregoing sub-sections are concerned with four aspects of organisational involvement : range of membership, extent of participation in organisational programmes, experience of travel and addressing groups of people. Each of these items has a three level participation score of High, Middle and Low. It is to be noted that most participants fall in the low-level participation score on range of membership, travel and addressing groups while the majority score 'High' in extent of activity in organisational programmes. The general organisational involvement of respondents shows that most respondents are fairly actively engaged in one or two socio-political organisations at the village level. The majority of them are not in the habit of travelling outside the village for meetings or organisational programmes. About 50 per cent of the respondents have had one or more experiences of speaking to groups, some in the absolute informality of a village mahila mandal, others in the formal atmosphere of an election campaign. Women who live very close to or in district headquarters tend to have a wide range of membership in socio-political organisations. Some of these are of the ambitious type who seek occasions of widening their spheres of social contact and influence as compared with the average respondent in the sample, who prefers the security of her village home and who accepts a social assignment outside only as a secondary commitment.

Participation in camps/training courses

As a measure to educate and thus prepare a more enlightened cadre of leadership in panchayat bodies, several training centres have been established under the auspices of the Government in various districts of Maharashtra. These centres are expected to conduct periodic training courses for members of panchayat bodies. There are also training centres for women, originally started to train gram sevikas and mukhya sevikas in the Community Development Blocks but which have now expanded the scope of their services to cover all sections of rural women. The State Social Welfare Advisory Board through its Family and Child Welfare projects in rural areas also conducts special activities for women under the Griha Kalyan Kendra Programme. Agricultural universities also conduct training courses for various groups, including women, in rural areas. These courses are of varying duration from one day to a month and they cover theory as well as practice in different fields: leadership, panchayati raj, home-crafts for women, agriculture.

The readiness of a woman to participate in a camp indicates her desire to learn and be part of a group. Since attendance at these camps is optional, a woman who decides to join in, manifests a desire to expose herself to a wider experience of learning and of socialisation. Attendance at camps may thus be considered as a form of increased social participation on the part of respondents.

The question that arises here is the availability of such opportunities for women all over the districts of Maharashtra. It is not known which districts are more favoured in this regard nor how many women can use the opportunities offered. Since background data on these points is not available, an exploratory study such as this has to probe to get a general feel of the situation. This investigation into the participation of respondents in camps or training courses has a two-fold purpose :

(i) to see how far respondents use the facilities that are being offered and thereby measure the degree of their social participation in this regard.

(ii) to see why respondents may have a high or low level of participation in this area.

The data collected on this issue may be depicted in the following tables under the headings :

(a) Number of camps/courses attended.
(b) Subjects treated.
(c) Location of camps.
(d) Benefits gained from camps/training courses.

Number of camps/courses attended

Assuming that voluntary participation at camps or such like training courses indicates a tendency towards wider social participation, the respondents have been given points which increase according to the number of camps attended. Lower scores, therefore, indicate a low or nil degree of participation. Table 5.7 shows the number of camps which respondents have attended :

TABLE 5.7 : **Number of camps/courses attended**

Number of Camps	Score	Rating	No. of Respondents
1. None	0	Low (L)	89
2. One camp	1	Middle (M)	37
3. Two camps	2	High (H)	10
4. Three camps and more	3	High (H)	8
		Total	144

Table 5.7 shows that the majority of 89 respondents have not attended any camps. Only a small number of 18 respondents have participated in 2 or more camps while the larger number of 37 have attended only one camp.

In the case of a couple of respondents from the Bombay Division, whose education and social experience are very wide, attendance at camps as a measure of social participation becomes superfluous. Their cases serve to show the limits of this tool of measurement, in their particular situation.

Subjects treated at camps/courses

Table 5.8 gives an idea of the subjects that have been dealt with for the benefit of women attending the camps or courses:

TABLE 5.8 : **Subjects treated at camps/training courses**

	Subject	No. of Respondents
1.	Subjects of interest to women e.g. Home-management, Child-care, Home-crafts	28
2.	General information on Panchayati Raj, Duties of Members	26
3.	Agricultural Methods	7
4.	Not Applicable	89

The subjects of interest to women, as mentioned in Table 5.8 have been dealt with mainly at Mahila Shibirs conducted by the Griha Kalyan Kendra which tailors the course content to suit various sectors of rural women. The original plan for these Mahila Shibirs was to have a residential camp but women found it too difficult to be away from their homes for a fortnight continuously, mainly because of family responsibilities.

Some respondents said that they had attended one-day camps in their own or in neighbouring villages. These camps mostly concern agricultural practices. A couple of respondents from the Jalgaon District attended longer camps on agricultural methods and they in turn started Discussion Groups for women (Krishi Mahila Charcha Mandal) at the local level. At present, the effort is to hold a camp here and there. There is no evidence of follow-up action. The women as a rule, prefer to attend camps specifically for women.

Location of camps

This item seeks to locate the places where camps were held, as being far from or near the respondents' residence.

TABLE 5.9 : **Location of camp-site**

Location	No. of Respondents
1. Village of residence/neighbouring village	7
2. Another Taluka/District Headquarters	33
3. Out of Respondents' District	15
4. Not applicable	89
Total	144

Table 5.9 shows that most of the camps were held in taluka or district headquarters. A central meeting place has to be found with amenities for boarding, lodging, theoretical instruction and group discussion. The taluka centre is usually better equipped with transport facilities than interior areas.

Camps held at a distance from villages, obliging women to stay out of their homes for several days together, make it difficult to reach out to women at the village grass-roots. A respondent was answering the questions asked by the researcher in the presence of her husband. When the researcher asked why the respondent was not able to attend any camps for women, the husband interrupted : "If she goes, who will make chappatis for me ?" Thus to ensure their participation, the camp-site should be closer to their home or convenient transport be made available. Three respondents had wanted to participate in organised camps but due to very poor attendance, the camps were cancelled. These instances show the need of a more attentive organisation of training programmes for women in rural areas.

Benefits gained from camps/training courses

The respondents found it difficult to specify benefits gained from these camps and, therefore, only general observations about their answers will be made. Most of the respondents who had attended camps felt that they gained in knowledge and self-confidence in a group. They were enthused by the new information they received in home-management and home-crafts which they did try to put into practice. A few respondents were able to share their knowledge with other women of the village as in the case of the Discussion Clubs for women in Jalgaon District. One respondent spoke of the opportunity she got to speak to a group during the camp and she felt very happy to think she did something she never felt confident to do before.

Four respondents who are more educated and more socially active than the majority of respondents attended camps as staff-members or guest-speakers. However, of the larger number of respondents whose level of education and social experience is limited, participation in camps or training courses of the kind mentioned above were found to give women a sense of satisfaction in acquiring knowledge and finding greater interest in the daily chores of their lives. Some women spoke appreciatively of the 'socialising' experience of the camp thus reaffirming the aspect of "self-confidence" which is the most important value of the camp experience.

The most frequent reasons for not attending any camps, were those of domestic duties, farm or agricultural responsibility and lack of information regarding the camp. The fact that women do not receive sufficient about the holding of camp seems to indicate either that very few such opportunities exist, or that the machinery to inform and encourage women to attend these courses, is inadequate. By and large respondents felt that camp or training courses for women are a desirable activity for women's development.

PERCEPTION OF MEMBERSHIP ROLE

This sub-section marks an attempt to portray the view that respondents have about their own role in the ZP/PS and what could help them to perform better. The questions touch mainly upon the representation of women in the ZP/PS under the following heads :

(a) Present pattern of representation.
(b) Experience gained as member of ZP/PS.
(c) Difficulties encountered.
(d) Desire to continue in office.
(e) Suggestions.
(f) Summary.

Present pattern of representation

The respondents were asked to express whether they were in agreement with the present statute of having one woman on the Panchayat

Samiti and two on the Zilla Parishad, if no women came up by election on these bodies. Table 5.10 shows the pattern of responses :

TABLE 5.10 : **Respondents' views on present pattern of representation**

Response	No. of Respondents
1. Satisfied	13
2. Need for more seats	129
3. No opinion	2
Total	144

Table 5.10 shows that the overwhelming majority of 129 respondents (89% of the sample) are not satisfied with the present quota of seats allotted to women and desire to have more representation on the ZP/PS. Those who express satisfaction reflect two points of view : a conservative one which says that there is no need for more women to move about in public life and a progressive view which feels that the effectiveness of representation is not in the number of members but in the quality selected. The latter group posed the question: "What is the use of having many silent or '*ho mannar bais*' as representatives ?"

Since many of the respondents had expressed a desire to have more seats for women on ZP/PS, bodies, they were asked to explain their reasons. Many found it difficult to express their views. Most of those who are on ZP/PS bodies would feel more confident to participate in the presence of more women members. Some saw representation as an opportunity for personal development because they gained more information about things and situations around them. This gain is not excluded from the development envisaged in the statute even though its scope may be limited. In effect, social awareness is the first step towards social participation. A group of about 7 respondents mentioned proportionate representation for men and women saying that society should function as in a family. Their analogy was : "Can a bullock-cart run on one wheel ? Can a family run well with only one parent ?" If women account for a certain percentage of the population, then they should be represented in proportion to their numbers. The contribution of men and women is needed for things to work out smoothly. The modalities of how this proportionate representation should be worked out was not discussed. A couple of respondents suggested the formation of women's constituencies for the purpose of electing women on these bodies. A few respondents did not seem to favour the provision of special representation for women and thought that they should go in for equal competition with men.

Experience gained as ZP/PS member

This is a rather wide-ranging area and respondents found it difficult to specify the gains or otherwise of their experience. Some leads were given to the respondents and their responses is shown in Table 5.11 :

TABLE 5.11 : **Experience gained as ZP/PS member**

Response	No. of Respondents
1. Do not feel so uncomfortable now to sit at the meetings in the presence of so many men	87
2. Have a wider interest in community problems	70
3. Able to speak when asked	42
4. Feel a greater responsibility to engage in some service for the community	34
5. Able to travel alone for meetings	8
6. Have widened social contacts	7
7. Learnt about the politics of such bodies	6
8. Did not gain much	11

Table 5.11 shows that the respondents gave more than one response to express the gains they experienced in their membership role. The general trend in responses 1, 3 and 5 is the gain in personal confidence; the trend in responses 2, 4, 6, 7 is the gain in social awareness. Both these trends show that a healthy development is taking place among the women representatives of ZP/PS. It was very rewarding to listen to the personal experience of each interviewee especially those who had become involved in their role by the end of their term of office.

Most women said that the experience of sitting as the sole woman at a Panchayat Samiti meeting was rather uncomfortable in the beginning. To dare say anything in the group was out of the question at that time. However, as the responses in Table 5.11 show, the initial discomfort was no longer felt by some and to a much lesser extent by others. Some admitted that though they felt more at ease to sit at these meetings, they still felt diffident to speak. One of the interviewees who lived hardly 5 kilometres away from a Panchayat Samiti office did not come to the office for the interview because her husband who usually accompanies her to and from the Samiti meetings was away. An illiterate respondent replied in picturesque language about what she felt at the start and after five years of membership : "In the beginning I used to feel as if someone was pulling me by the ears and taking me to the meeting but now I can pull anyone else's ears' ! Many spoke about the desire they felt of doing some service for the community as a result of listening in at ZP/PS meetings. Hearing the issues that were discussed, they began to see and understand problems beyond the walls of their own homes.

Underlying nearly all the responses is perceptible a growing urge on the part of respondents to be able to meet the challenge of a new social role. To be alone, to sit as the sole female representative in a male-dominated meeting, to express one's view when requested, are small but significant projections of women-members which are not reflected in minutes of meetings nor in the records of panchayat achievements. These constitute the real seeds of hope and promise for the development of the rural woman. Her growth in self-confidence as a person and as a member of the rural community is the spring-board of further development and if this is what statute regarding women's representation has been able to generate, it may claim to have achieved much of its purpose.

Desire to continue in office

This question was asked in order to re-confirm how positively or negatively respondents felt about their membership role.

Fifty-two per cent of the respondents have come to regard panchayat membership as a source of prestige, bringing with it many privileges in spite of responsibilities. Identifying with the attitude of their milieu they also treat it as a position of power, particularly when respected male-members of the family hold panchayat status. They would wish to be nominated for one term after another.

A small group of 15 respondents who feel that others should be given a chance are among the more progressive thinkers in the sample. Most of them have been active participants in panchayat bodies even before the present term and they feel it not fair for the same people to continue long in office. Younger people must also be given a chance to gain in this experience. These respondents have a personal sense of achievement and they are happy with what they have been able to do as well as with the recognition they have obtained, hence they are ready to make room for others.

ROLE-PERFORMANCE AS MEMBER OF ZP/PS

This sub-section focusses on the role-performance of the respondent in her specific capacity as member of the ZP/PS, whereas the first sub-section reviewed the pattern of general social participation in the rural community. To assess the respondents' actual functioning in her membership role, the following items will be considered :

(a) Duration of office.
(b) Procedure of appointment to the ZP/PS.
(c) Attendance at meetings.
(d) Interest in women's welfare.
(e) Speaking at meetings.
(f) Type of assistance rendered and respondents' personal involvement.
(g) Contact with SC/ST.

Duration of office

It is proposed under this item to see whether the respondent held the appointment of membership to the ZP/PS for the full five-year term of office. An overwhelming majority of 134 respondents (93 per cent of the sample) held office for the full tenure of 5 years. Of these, Table 5.1 shows that 80 respondents had held previous terms of office in panchayat bodies. About 20 respondents held office for a duration of 10 to 15 years either at the Gram Panchayat, Samiti or Zilla Parishad levels. This continuance in office on the part of senior women, was resented by a young respondent of 28 years who insisted on breaking the tradition of allowing certain women to continue for 2 and 3 terms of office. She felt that affluence had much to do with these decisions. She would have liked to challenge the established custom by standing for election but again to set up an election campaign was an expensive affair and she could not afford it in her personal capacity. She sought to align herself with a political party which would support her in her ambition to occupy the women's seat in the P.S.

Procedure of appointment to the ZP/PS

The representation of women on the Zilla Parishad in Maharashtra is laid down as : "two women co-opted if the directly elected member do not include a woman or women". On the Panchayat Samiti, the clause concerning women's representation reads thus : "Co-option of one woman residing in the block if such representation is not already include ......". (Govt. of Maharashtra; 1971 : 15). Women may thus be represented on the ZP/PS either by direct election or by co-option. In the election procedure she competes equally with other in the constituency selected and faces the risks involved. In the event of there being no elected women either on the ZP or PS, the president of the ZP or chairman of the PS, proposes the names of women who are judged to be suitable candidates and the members express by vote or otherwise their acceptance or not of the name proposed. Most often it is the dominant party in the ZP or PS which gets its nominee selected. Table 5.12 shows the position of elected or co-opted women candidates in the ZP/PS of Maharashtra.

TABLE 5.12 : **Region-wise choice of women members on ZP/PS**

Procedure	No. of Respondents				
	Vidarbha	Marathwada	Pune Div.	Bombay Div.	Total
1. By election	1	0	1	4	6
2. By co-option	53	22	34	29	138
Total	54	22	35	33	144

Table 5.12 shows that a tiny fraction of barely 4 per cent of the sample (6 respondents) have successfully contested elections to the ZP and stand as elected representatives at the ZP and PS levels.

The Bombay Division has the highest number of elected representatives. All the other representatives (96 per cent) are co-opted.

On the face of it, co-option seems to imply a certain forced collaboration. Women do not come forward spontaneously in the normal election procedure but they have to be drawn into the body by co-option. Is this an indication of women's general backwardness to participate in political life ? Is this a manifestation of backwardness among the rural women of Maharashtra ?

To answer the second question, one would need to compare the figures in Table 5.12 with similar figures of women's representation in other states of the country. These figures are not available. As for the first question one may say that women do not generally enter the field of political leadership both in India as well as on the International scene. In the Scandinavian countries, where women are said to have a high social status, actual political participation is modest and few women are nominated or elected to political office. (Patai; 1967: 445). Women in political office are few in any country of the world. (Ward; 1963 : 73). If such is the case for all women, even those exposed to more modernised ways of life, it is true to say that women in rural areas are more hesitant to come forward and occupy prominent public positions such as those in the ZP/PS. The traditional view has always assigned to women the more hidden role of service in the home, a role to which they have become attuned. Thus they have remained far from the public eye, from the wider circles of power and influence which are important factors in an election campaign. They cannot project themselves in the kind of activity where the ability to publicise oneself and one's achievements is a major requirement. Veiled at home, they cannot suddenly stand the gaze of crowds. Today the success of an election is not merely the success of an individual, it is the success of the party to publicise, make attractive propaganda and sway the electorate even pressurising people by various means. One of the respondents who stood for elections to the ZP said that it was only because the party prevailed upon her to stand, assuring her that they would undertake responsibility for the election campaign. "They did everything—canvassing for votes and spending". Her own expense in the process was minimal. The respondent was a respected woman in the locality and had a good record of service to the people in her area. Her case shows that if the party decides to sponsor a woman-candidate for the elections, they can do so. The initiative, therefore, is not merely an individual decision, it is a party affair. How far do parties feel they should encourage women-candidates ? The answer may be found partly in the following illustration.

A respondent who was ambitious and had successfully contested previous elections, said that her party had prevailed upon her during the last ZP election, not to stand for elections because her winning the election would deprive the party of an extra seat in the ZP as well as the PS. In case the women-contestant is elected, there is no room for co-option and a co-opted member enjoys the same privileges of voting, as elected members. Political parties, therefore, utilise the statute regarding co-option as a means of gaining votes and strengthening their party-position in the panchayat body. One of the elected representatives to the ZP related to the researcher how she was wooed by three political parties to stand for the State Assembly Elections but she refused to ride on the tickets of parties about which she felt disillusioned. In this instance, her refusal to stand for elections could manifest a greater sense of responsibility, hence a higher level of development among women.

The above instances show the important roles that political parties play in the election and co-option of women in panchayat bodies. The statute aims at the development of women but the statute is in the hands of politicians to manipulate. In our days it would seem as if the obsession of political parties is power-retention, not the aspiration after an ideology embodied in a well-defined strategy for the development of weaker sections. In such an atmosphere, women too become pawns to keep people in power because as yet women's ability to function independently has remained stunted. How many Panchayat Samitis and Zilla Parishads have co-opted mere "yes" women ('*ho mannar bai*') because those in power are more interested in her vote rather than in her contribution towards women's development. The data show that women representatives are generally co-opted for various political reasons at the ZP/PS levels, and the vastness of the area makes it impossible for many to function effectively at district and block levels. It is the Gram Panchayat (GP) that holds more promise for women's effective participation in rural areas. Though the GP does not fall within the purview of this study, the researcher came in contact with women-members of the GP during the course of data-collection. Some had even held the office of sarpanch. At the village level it is easier for women to participate in social life. The members of the GP are known to the respondent and there is an element of familiarity which helps her to feel more comfortable in her membership role. Moreover, meetings are held at a stone's throw from the house so that the difficulty of transport and overnight halts is largely eliminated.

Thus the fact that only 6 women have been elected among the 50 representatives in the Zilla Parishads of Maharashtra cannot in itself be interpreted as a sign of backwardness among rural women.

Attendance at meetings

With regard to regularity of attendance, one may observe that the vast majority of respondents consider their attendance at ZP/PS meetings as regular. Irregularity at meetings is caused by ill-health or transport problems especially during the monsoon. No one is absent for prolonged periods because of the ruling that any member who is absent for three meetings at a stretch without prior information as to the reason for absence, is disqualified from membership. At the same time there is a material advantage to attendance at meetings, in terms of one's travelling allowance which may be obtained only on signing the register. It was related to the researcher that the practice of sending the register to the house of the absent woman-representative is not infrequent. Such practices, to say the least, make no contribution to improving the quality of women's participation as members. The researcher did find, however, a couple of respondents against whom cases of suspension had been introduced because the BDO and other officials observed that their attendance was very irregular.

The difficulty of transport during the monsoon season is great specially in those areas which do not have a proper approach road. In a particular case, a respondent walked through 3 miles of slush and waited for 2 hours for a bus to go to the Samiti office where the researcher awaited her. After having waited for the respondent up to 2 hours beyond the appointed time, the BDO kindly undertook to drive the researcher in his jeep to her house situated about 15 kilometres away from the Samiti office. The jeep drove on slowly, oscillating precariously on rugged, rain-washed paths, sometimes diving into soft mud and sometimes bouncing on stony mounds. Finally after an hour of jeep-rattling it arrived at the bus-stop near the respondent's residence to find her sitting patiently on a boulder, waiting for a bus. She had undertaken to make the journey to the Samiti office only because the BDO had sent a peon the previous evening to accompany her to the office the next morning. This depicts to some extent the practical difficulties involved with communication between the Samiti office and individual members. These difficulties apply to all in the rural set-up but cultural practices render the process more complex for women.

Interest in women's welfare

The question on women's welfare was motivated by the following considerations :

(1) to find out how far the welfare of women as a subject figured at the ZP/PS meetings, from the experience of the respondents ;

(2) to find out the respondent's own view of the subject of women's welfare as being of much or little consequence in the policies and programmes of the ZP/PS.

In response to the first question, 96 respondents said that the subject was rarely discussed at ZP/PS meeting whereas 46 found that the matter did come up occasionally and 2 members were at a loss to reply.

The following is a tabulation of the reasons given by respondents for the lower priority accorded to women's welfare :

TABLE 5.13 : **Reasons for limited attention to women's welfare**

Reasons	No. of respondents
1. Lack of concern on the part of men	50
2. Lack of initiative on the part of women	48
3. No necessity of discussing the issue separately	32
4. Unable to express an opinion	14
Total	144

It would appear from Table 5.13 that the subject of women's welfare as such does not figure significantly during ZP/PS meetings. The most frequently expressed reason is the indifference of male members to the issue of women's development. One respondent described the male attitude thus : "Women's problems are too small for them. They have big problems : building of roads, construction of taps, etc". It is not that the construction of roads nor the provision of water are less important but an all-round effort to develop the rural areas requires that attention be paid to developing the persons who compose rural society not the least among whom are women. An example of what is specifically a problem among women is the education of girls which is low in rural areas. A couple of respondents related how indifferent the male reaction was when they tried to request help for their Mahila Mandals at the PS meetings. To one respondent, the answer was : "Keep your Mahila Mandal aside" (*Tumche mahila mandal bazula theva*). Another respondent expressed her disappointment at not being able to find a suitable place for their meetings though their Mahila Mandal had been in existence for the last 25 years. In one district where the chairman of the ZP was a woman, she ensured a greater participation on the part of women by co-opting 2 more women from the district in 2 committees of the ZP. This was the only instance where 5 women from the district functioned at the ZP level. The Chairman (a woman) who had considerable experience of working in the Panchayati Raj structure, said that generally speaking women workers even in the position of BDO felt that men do not show much interest in women's programmes. The researcher's own contacts with women workers confirmed this view. One of the more active respondents who had successfully contested elections earlier felt that she would never be given a chance to occupy the position of Chairman of the Panchayat Samiti, because she is a woman. Another respondent said that the taking of the register to the woman's house for her signature when she did not attend meetings showed the low esteem they have both for the woman and her position in the GP.

A fair number of 32 respondents (Table 5.13) felt that there was no need of discussing the issue as a separate subject because it was covered in discussion on general development, e.g., health, family planning, education. The ZP Social Welfare Committee on which the women representatives are usually nominated, also attends to the distribution of aid for backward classes, as well as for women's welfare. One respondent said that it was not so much women's problems but the problems of the poor which hardly receive the attention they should get. Those respondents belonging to the more developed parts of rural areas located closer to urban areas, felt that women in their talukas were fairly active at PS meetings. Their interests get looked after in the normal course of things so there is no need of making special provision for women's welfare. The latter belong mostly to the Bombay Division group.

A small minority of 14 respondents (Table 5.13) could hardly follow the proceedings of the ZP/PS meetings and were, therefore, unable to express any definite opinion to the question asked on women's welfare.

It would seem that women's interests are not adequately represented at ZP/PS meetings partly because women themselves fail to show adequate interest, and many hardly find it necessary to give the subject separate treatment.

Speaking at meetings

This item apparently probes a very superficial facet of social participation, yet, it represents an important stage of growth for rural women. As remarked in the introduction to this chapter, this study is not interested in establishing norms of assessment which may suit urbanised societies but have no applicability to rural areas. To be able to speak at a meeting may be regarded by women at the level of MLA's or MP's as the most elementary form of participation in a membership role but for a woman steeped in the rural tradition it may mark a courageous leap forward in her social development. It constitutes a real break-through to have them sitting, amidst a group of men and expressing their views. In order to assess how far women were able to speak at ZP/PS meetings a question was asked to that effect. A better way of finding this out would have been to sit through a ZP/PS meeting and observe the participation of the respondents. This, however, would have necessitated the obtaining of a time-table of all the ZP/PS meetings in the State and the possibility of travelling to various talukas situated all over the districts whenever a PS meeting was held. This was impossible to realise in practice with the resources available to the researcher, who was, therefore, content to obtain the women's own response to this question as in the case of all the other criteria of social participation. The participation of respondents by speaking at meetings has been taken as one of the measurable criteria of social participation ; hence, the responses have been given scores according to the extent of participation. The researcher observed that the self-assessment of respondents was consistent with their overall behaviour and pattern of involvement. Table 5.14 : illustrates the frequency of speaking at ZP/PS meetings.

TABLE 5.14 : **Frequency of speaking at meetings**

Response	Score	Rating		No. of Respondents	%
1. Often	2	High	(H)	37	26
2. Rarely	1	Middle	(M)	80	55
3. Never	0	Low	(L)	27	19
		Total		144	100

Table 5.14 shows that 37 respondents (26%) score "High", the majority of 80 (55%) score in the "Middle" category and the smallest number of 27 (19%) are in the "low" participation group. The line of distinction between "rare" and "never" is difficult to identify. In many cases, the women speak only at the time of voting on an issue, when they have to show their hands in an expression of assent or dissent. In fact, many just adopt the stance laid down by the party. One of the respondents told the researcher that she never speaks at meetings, though the researcher actually found her to be a pleasant, sociable type of person. Her father was an "izzar", a big landowner and a man of repute. In her childhood and youth she never appeared before men without a purdah and so now even though she had got used to sitting at PS meetings in the presence of so many men, she feels very inhibited to speak. If she has anything to say, she gives it in writing.

On the whole, the social participation of respondents as measured by this particular indicator of ability to speak at meetings, is on the low side.

Type of assistance rendered and respondents' personal involvement

It is proposed under this title, to find out how far women are involved in assistance or action programmes undertaken by the ZP/PS and to indicate the areas of involvement. The touchstone of success as a member in the panchayat structure is the implementation of effective, developmental aid programmes among the local population at the village, taluka or district levels. This may call for resourcefulness on the part of panchayat members but most often what is required is the ability of members to apply approved aid-programmes with budgeted allotments to the needs of people in specific areas.

This action-oriented role of members calls for direct encounters with people, a sensitivity to people's problems and an awareness of the help available through the panchayat structure. The ability to implement developmental programmes depends largely on the kind of rapport that exists between the member and those who hold power (in terms of official authority or economic superiority) in the community. Often a member may not need to make direct contacts with officials on behalf of applicants because a signature on an application form can easily open access to the resources available.

Today, the programmes of assistance whether in cash or kind can be implemented only through a maze of printed forms, written statements, true copies, rubber stamps which are quite confusing to uneducated people. Rural women, the majority of whom have remained illiterate and uneducated, would hardly be in a position to write an application, leave alone scrutinise its validity. In this sense, their ability to be involved in programmes of assistance would necessarily be limited. However, applications for aid must be recommended by a member of the ZP/PS of the area concerned. For a recommendation to be effective, the ascriptive status of the member comes into play, and women may be effective in this way. How worthy is the applicant for receiving the aid, is another question. However, it is likely that the participation of women representatives may be limited to affixing a signature or thumb-impression for an applicant, at the behest of her husband or some other influential member of the local community. There may be some women who have an innate ability for leadership and who are able to mobilise resources as well as be personally involved in the channelisation of aid according to felt needs. The question that poses itself is : what aid-giving programmes of the ZP/PS are women representatives involved in and what is the extent of their personal involvement. These are only the broad lines of a question that could be studied in greater depth.

The present investigation touches only upon the fringe of the pattern of women's participation in assistance programmes undertaken by the ZP/PS. The information gathered and the subsequent analysis are based on impressions and facts communicated to the researcher by the respondents themselves. There could be a more objective verification of the facts. The extensiveness of the study made it impossible to explore each area in greater depth.

Having met each interviewee personally either in her home or in the ZP/PS office, and conversed with her for a duration of one to two hours, it was possible for the researcher to form an impression of the personal interest and extent of involvement of the respondent in the action-oriented programmes of ZP/PS. To bind rural women who faced a researcher for the first time in their lives, to answer details of 'when', 'how', 'how much' was too much to expect within the limited time available. What was more important was to create an atmosphere of confidence in which the respondent could share spontaneously the things she had been able to do or not in the context asked. The researcher was, therefore, satisfied with gathering what respondents could recollect sometimes on their own, sometimes with the help of those around, on the type of help they had been able to give to people or where their efforts had failed.

The participation of respondents in assistance programmes of the ZP/PS will be seen under :

(1) Requests for aid.
(2) Types of assistance given.
(3) Personal involvement.

Requests for aid

With regard to this item, a large majority of respondents (78%) do receive requests for aid whereas 22 per cent of the respondents said that they do not receive such requests. Many of the latter said that they prefer not to involve themselves in this area.

Several questions remain to be answered: Do the requests come directly to the respondent or through the husband or some other media? To what extent is the intervention of the woman sought by the local community? A Harijan respondent said that the sabhapati was not favourably inclined towards her and seemed to have ignored a request she had made. She had resolved not to ask for aid again. The local people seeing that she had no influence, did not approach her with their requests. Such incidents give rise to a spate of questions on the role of the woman nominated on the ZP/PS and the local community. It is an area worth investigating further if one is genuinely interested in the kind of social contribution that women can make through these bodies. For the present, it is seen that nearly one-fourth of the sample is inactive as far as involvement in programmes of assistance are concerned. The others who claim some measure of involvement may have very varied patterns of intervention from the almost passive to the very active. The researcher has attempted to give a quantitative assessment to the varied shades of involvement, in No. 3 of this section.

Type of assistance given

Under this type it is seen that the various types of assistance that respondents were able to make use of for the needs of different groups or individuals in the local community, as depicted in Table 5.15.

TABLE 5.15 : **Type of assistance**

Type of Assistance	No. of Respondents
1. Aid for Mahila Mandals, Balwadis	63
2. Agricultural inputs for farmers	42
3. Aid for essential services in villages (roads, drinking water, school building)	34
4. Aid for house-construction and repair	32
5. Aid for self-employment schemes	32
6. Recommendations for transfer of teachers	25
7. Promotion of activities for youth	3
8. None	33
Total	264

The types of assistance as listed above form an impressive list of the kind of help that is being rendered to the local community through panchayat bodies. Even though Mahila Mandals and Balwadis figure high on the list, the types of assistance are for the most part economic, which is the basic need of rural communities today. The priorities featuring on the list are encouraging because they respond to very definite areas of need in rural areas. As such the replies of many interviewees reveal that they are in touch with the actual situation, even though the respondents are in a more privileged position than those among whom the need exists.

Table 5.15 shows that the largest number of respondents were able to render assistance mainly in the area of development for women and children. This assistance has generally taken place in the form of grants, equipment or getting personnel to work for Mahila Mandals and Balwadis. Some respondents also took interest in procuring various facilities to improve the education of children in primary schools. Other forms of aid were effected mainly by signing the application forms of people desirous of obtaining help. In many instances, the requests came through the husband and when he recommends, the wife signs unquestionably. It is also to be observed that most respondents were able to render service mainly in their own villages even though they might be on bodies at the taluka and district levels. Since most women on the Zilla Parishads are co-opted in the Social Welfare Committees, much of the aid distributed was directed towards the SC/ST which are the special focus of these committees.

As mentioned earlier, the aid given by the ZP/PS has to pass through a number of written formalities which demand a conversant knowledge of reading, writing, accounts. The rural farmer is himself at a loss and becomes dependent on the staff of officers or educated persons to find his way out of situations. How much greater is the dependence of the rural woman who, besides the handicap of illiteracy cannot move about freely in public ! No wonder then that the majority of them prefer to leave this aspect of work to their husbands or sons who are generally more educated than they. No wonder also that many women feel that their maximum contribution is to sign the register of attendance at meetings without even waiting for the duration of the meeting !

It cannot be helped that greater efficiency in the administration and follow-up of social services demands the keeping of records and increased secretarial competence. It follows, however, that members of the ZP/PS will have to be prepared for the role expected of them and be helped to acquire the necessary competence. If this preparation of members is not taken seriously, the educated few will have their hands strengthened by the incompetence of the majority. Such concentration of power can defeat the aspiration for democratic decentralization which is the underlying inspiration of Panchayati Raj. The preparation of leaders in Panchayati Raj is necessary in the cases of both men and women but in the case of women, the plea is stronger because their social development lags far behind that of men. Unless a determined effort is made to bridge the gap between the expected social performance of women and their actual situation, the statute regarding women's representation may become a meaningless prescription.

In the personal contacts that the researcher had with each interviewee either in her own home surrounded by members of her family or in the Samiti office where other members of the ZP or PS were present, the researcher was able to see the personal involvement of the respondent in the action-oriented programmes of the ZP/PS. Some women actually took the researcher to certain places in the village where a well had been dug or an approach road made ; some spoke animatedly about the work undertaken during their term of office ; some just shook their heads and said they had not done anything ; several said that their husbands took care of things. A few realised their responsibility as members but family duties made it impossible to respond. Thus the researcher was able to form an impression about their personal involvement in the programme. Involvement leads to actual intervention or effective action in the securing or utilization of aid. The effective action taken by respondents in the procurement of aid or in the implementation of a project connected with ZP/PS is termed as "personal intervention". It connotes action taken with the personal initiative of the respondent at least at some point of the aid-giving process, as against the "leave it for others to do" attitude. The researcher's assessment is made after personally interviewing each of the respondents. Each one has been given scores which correspond to a ranking of High, Middle or Low level of personal intervention. There would be other ways of checking on the personal intervention of members, for example, by interviewing officials or other members of the ZP/PS or even people from the local community but here again it was not possible to use all these techniques within the scope of this one study. The researcher has checked the scores on this item against the other criteria of social participation so as to assure that there is internal consistency in the pattern of scores. Table 5.16 gives the range of personal intervention as an indicator of social participation with regard to the types of assistance rendered through the ZP/PS.

Table 5.16 shows that the group marked 'low' covering items 1 (31) and 2 (44) adds to a total of 75 which accounts for 52 per cent of the sample. The respondents in the extreme categories of "none" and "high" were comparatively easy to recognise. Those in the categories of "some" and "fair" have a less clearly marked pattern. What is important to observe is that 48 per cent (30+39 =69) of the sample falls in the "high" and "middle" categories of participation which dispels the popular myth that women on panchayat bodies are quite inactive. The respondents in the Bombay Division are characterised by having the highest percentages

TABLE 5.16 : **Extent of personal intervention in assistance programmes (Region-wise distribution)**

Rating	Score	No. of Respondents				
		Vidharba	Marathwada	Pune Div.	Bombay Div.	Total
1. None (Low)	0	14	3	3	11	31
2. Some (Low)	1	20	8	11	5	44
3. Fair (Middle)	2	10	5	11	4	30
4. High (High)	3	10	6	10	13	39
		54	22	35	33	144

of respondents in the two extreme categories of "high" and "low". This is not the only case of the Bombay Division showing extremes in development norms because of the varied levels of development in its district population structure. The Pune Division shows a more equal distribution of respondents in the 3 upper categories. The scores marked above will be added with the scores of other criteria on social participation so that the respondent gets a collective score on this variable which can then be measured against other independent variables. It is well-worth recounting an instance related by a respondent which clarifies what is meant by personal intervention and highlights the rich contribution that women can make to the quality of 'development' debates. A respondent, member of the PS a widow of 40 years who had to shoulder a heavy responsibility with 6 children to support, was sitting quietly through a PS meeting. A heated debate was on between the two major parties as to whether a small bridge should be constructed over a '*nalla*' in the village. As the confusion mounted, the respondent who had never spoken before could not contain herself on what she considered an important issue. "For the sake of all our children who go to school and daily face the danger of crossing flooded *nalla* I ask that the bridge be built". There was silence......the discussion was ended. No party could dare refuse the plea of a mother anxious about the physical safety of her children and reflecting the anxiety experienced by many mothers in the village, who see their children wading through the *nalla* on their way to and from school everyday. If only such examples could be multiplied and women on the ZP/PS could help to focus interest on the real human problems in development.

Contact with SC/ST population

The interests of weaker sections of the population, namely women and SC/ST are represented by the co-option of members belonging to these groups. Moreover, women are usually nominated on the Social Welfare Committees of Zilla Parishads which are concerned specially with the welfare of the backward classes. Since the national effort today is oriented towards drawing the economically under-privileged classes into the mainstream of national life, anyone who holds a position of formal leadership in a development-oriented body like that of the panchayat, is expected to consider the needs of this sector in the local community. The question that arises is : How far do women in ZP/PS bodies reach out towards women or others in need from the SC/ST classes ? Before laying down norms to judge effective outreach, the researcher preferred to explore the present pattern of social contact between the respondents and the SC/ST population.

The majority of respondents being from the land-owning sector, they may contact the labourers working in their fields when they come to the house for their meals or other work but the contact is generally limited to the work-situation. About seven respondents said that they do not take any food or drink in the houses of SC/ST. In this respect, the panchayat structure has helped considerably to overcome some of these cultural hurdles. When asked about taking food in the houses of people from backward classes, a respondent replied : "In any case if the scheduled caste member hands us a cup of tea at the meeting, I cannot refuse".

The broad pattern of communication between respondents and the SC/ST groups may be described as impersonal and utilitarian, responding more to social pressures in the administration of aid rather than to any local sense of responsibility for their welfare. Attending flag-hoisting functions, religious and cultural celebrations may hardly require much of inter-personal communication. Family celebrations like weddings which admit of a more selective group may indicate more personalised relationships. Several higher-caste respondents said that they could eat together with people from SC/ST in a public *pandal* but not in the homes of the latter.

The paying of home-visits is largely motivated by personal gain on the part of the upper classes. Election campaigns are about the most frequent occasion. However, it has to be recognised that even the election campaigns arising out of the panchayat structure serve to forge greater rapport between the SC/ST and the upper castes/classes. The preparation for elections obliges those who aspire for power to recognise their dependence on the under-privileged sections whose existence might otherwise have been completely ignored or even trampled upon. A certain process of political education is involved with each contestant presenting his/her manifesto and the masses becoming conscious of their power to swing the vote in favour or against.

Yet another incentive to further contacts between the respondents and people of SC/ST is provided by the panchayat structure through the Zilla Parishad Social Welfare Committee which includes the women-members of the ZP. Special programmes of assistance are chalked out for backward classes and women representatives are involved in receiving applications from this section of people, examining the need and seeing that aid is properly utilised. This help given through the Social Welfare Committees has undoubtedly created a greater sense of responsibility and interest among respondents to know and reach out to the needs of the under-privileged sections of their local communities. Numerous are the instances cited by the respondents of helping Harijan families to acquire agricultural inputs, loans, materials for house-construction/house repair, grants for Mahila Mandals and Balwadis, wells for drinking water, for irrigation, self-employment schemes and even adult education classes. Few respondents may go to the extent of the Brahmin respondent who employed a Harijan girl in her kitchen but the process of change in the increased social contacts between high caste and SC/ST has been generated. While it appears as if there is an upsurge of communalism and casteism in the country today, one must also be able to appreciate the dents that panchayat bodies have been able to make in the rigid walls of caste-structures. How far can the letter of the law as contained in the handbooks of panchayat bodies and the Constitution of the country, become the spirit of a people, is the challenge for the future. It is certain that unless the higher classes/castes are able to shed their cultural prejudices against the SC/ST population and open opportunities for them to compete increasingly on an equal basis, the latter may always be treated "with reservation". The cards are in the hands of those who wield power on these bodies : are they interested in playing a fair game or do they limit themselves to lip-service uplift of the weaker sections?

Since the above is only an overview of responses that touched the fringe of the question on social participation in relation to SC/ST, no quantitative assessment is possible. This item is, therefore, not included among the criteria measuring the social participation of respondents. It could be an area of study by itself.

LEVELS OF SOCIAL PARTICIPATION

In sub-sections 2 and 3 of this chapter, a fairly detailed analysis has been made of various factors indicating the general participation in socio-political organisations as well as their specific participation as members of ZP/PS bodies. It is possible at this stage to draw from the analysis various measurable criteria of social participation and give each respondent a total score which is the sum of points scored in each indicator of social participation. The collective score will determine the general level of participation of the respondents. The criteria selected as indicators of social participation are shown in Table 5.17

TABLE 5.17 : **Index of Respondents' level of social participation**

Indicator	Scores		
	Low	Middle	High
1. Organisational membership	0, 1	2, 3	4+
2. Extent of participation in programmes	0, 1	2	3
3. Extent of travel tours	0	1	2
4. Addressing social groups	0	1	2
5. Attendance at camps	0, 1	2	3+
6. Speaking at PS/ZP meetings	0	1	2
7. Personal involvement in assistance programmes of PS/ZP	0, 1	2	3
Collective scores	0-4	5-12	13+

The respondents' collective scores showing their general level of social participation is given in Table 5.18.

TABLE 5.18 : **Levels of social participation**

Level		No. of Respondents	Percentage
Low	(0—4)	32	22
Middle	(5—12)	76	53
High	(13+)	36	25
	Total	144	100

The scores seen percentage-wise show that the majority of respondents have a middle level of participation. One-fourth of them are high participants and a little less than one-fourth score in the low-level group. In other words, 36 respondents are quite active as members of the ZP/PS as well as in other socio-political organisations at the village, taluka and district levels; 76 respondents are somewhat active mostly at the village level and 32 are almost inactive in the membership role.

Social participation and socio-economic background of respondents

The levels of participation may be understood in a more meaningful way if seen in relation with variables that are likely to influence the social performance of women in a rural society. It has been recognised earlier (Chapter 3) that women in rural society are very greatly influenced by the family, especially the male members who determine largely the course of their lives. We may ask : How far does the family influence the social participation of women ? The socio-economic status of the family constitutes part of the family influence. It is, therefore, proposed to take the elements that have been studied in the socio-economic background and see whether they are significantly related with participation. The scores on general social participation will be related with the following factors in the data :

(1) Ascriptive factors : Caste, land-holding, political influence, family educational status, husbands' education, age of respondent.

(2) Achievement factors : Respondents' education, social outlook.

(1) The following Table 5.19 shows the significance of relationship between social participation and various ascriptive factors in the socio-economic background of respondents.

The χ^2 test of significance and 'gamma' test of correlation have been used :

TABLE 5.19 : **Social participation and social status of respondents**

Independent Variable	Dependent Variable	χ^2 value	Significance	γ
1. Caste	Social Participation	9.80 d.f. 6	$P > .05$	.13
2. Land-holding	,, ,,	5.01 d.f. 4	$P > .05$	.13
3. Political Influence	,, ,,	1.4 d.f. 4	$P > .05$	.08
4. Family Educational Status	,, ,,	13.74 d.f. 4	$P < .01$	.41
5. Husband's Education	,, ,,	13.65 d.f. 4	$P < .01$	.40
6. Age of Respondent	,, ,,	14.19 d.f. 4	$P < .01$	.25

The χ^2 tests show that the participation of respondents is not significantly related to the factors of caste and land-holdings which constitute the symbols of traditional power in the rural set-up. Political influence which has been found to be significantly related to the above traditional symbols : caste and land-holdings is also not significantly related to the wife's participation. In fact, the gamma reveals an extremely low level of relationship. It has been seen in Table 3.20 that political influence and husband's education have a fairly high degree of correlation which indicates that the factor of political influence is related to the husband's performance, not to that of his wife. It is his political influence that determines her selection on the ZP/PS. It is also seen that his political influence does not significantly affect her participation as a member of the

ZP/PS. Political influence may thus be considered as achievement for the husband but it is a factor of ascription for the wife. The data in Table 5.19 thus indicates that the social participation of respondents is not significantly related to the ritual, economic and political status of the family.

With regard to family educational status as well as the educational status of the husband, Table 5.19 shows that there is a significant relationship between each of these two factors and the respondents' social participation. The educational tradition of a family appears to play an important role in determining the extent of social participation among women-members of ZP/PS. This may explain why respondents even those belonging to the high landowning castes but with a low level of education do not manifest a participation level that is higher than women of other castes. The tradition of Maratha Kshatriya and Kunbi caste-groups have generally not fostered a high performance in education and among women the inhibitions were much greater. Table 3.13 indicates that out of 44 high caste and high land owning families in the sample, 18 have a low educational status, 16 have a medium status and 10 have a high educational status.

Education which generally fosters more progressive thinking on the role of woman is thus seen to reduce the effect of traditional culture regarding women's participation in public. This finding is borne out by testing the significance of the relation between husband's education and wife's participation as shown in Table 5.19. The observation fits in with a tradition that expects a wife to fall in step with her husband in all respects, here it being the area of education and participation. At the same time the husband's desire to have an educated wife hastens the process of social change because education opens the way to greater participation among women at the community level.

Table 5.19 shows that age and social participation are significantly related. In the case of outlook, age did not feature as a significant factor of influence. As already remarked in the age-pattern of respondents (Ch. 3) rural society shows more regard to older women and allows them a greater freedom to participate in the social life of the community. The status of woman is at its best in the role of an experienced mother or mother-in-law. Young women are usually not seen outside the home and even in the home there are often restrictions regarding their behaviour in the presence of visitors, specially men. Attendance at ZP/PS meetings generally means a day's travel or an overnight stay. This is not easily permitted in the case of young women. Family responsibilities are greater among the younger group of women who are at the child-bearing stage and have small children to care for. Many women are not able to take up any active social responsibility outside the home till they have a daughter-in-law in the house.

Achievement factors

Having seen the social participation of respondents against the socio-economic background of the family, it is of interest to see their participation in relation to factors which give greater opportunity for personal ability to manifest itself, as for instance education and social outlook.

Education and social participation

The following is a cross-tabulation of the respondents' educational and participation levels :

TABLE 5.20 : **Education and participation**

Education \ Participation	H	M	L	T
H	11	1	0	12
M	19	39	11	69
L	6	36	21	63
Total	36	76	32	144

$\chi^2 = 39.83$; d.f.$=4$

$P < .01$

$\gamma = .62$

The χ^2 test evidently points to a high level of significance between education and social participation. The gamma test indicates a fairly high degree of correlation between the two factors, higher than the correlation between education and the family educational status (.41) as well as husband's education (.40). (Table 5.19). This shows that education has an important place in initiating women to feature in the public life of rural communities. The Table 5.20 shows that 6 women who have a low degree of education have a high participation level which indicates that active participation is not dependent merely on a high level of formal education. Just a primary level of education has been enough to enable several women to become leaders in their local communities. Yet, one cannot ignore the overall trend of the table which definitely indicates that nearly 67 per cent of the respondents with a low level of participation also have a low educational level, as also those with a high educational level score high in participation. At the primary level, there is not so much of imparting of knowledge as giving attention to literacy. One may say that literacy and 'socializing' are the main merits of primary education. Several women who have emerged as leaders in the rural set-up with just a primary level of education, show that the emergence of leadership is less a question of theoretical knowledge or educational degrees and more a question of confidence to do a minimum of reading and writing as well as to establish social contacts outside the home.

Social outlook and participation

The following is a cross-tabulation of the scores of respondents on social outlook and participation.

TABLE 5.21 : **Outlook and participation**

Outlook \ Participation	H	M	L	T
H	23	33	5	61
M	12	33	11	56
L	1	10	16	27
Total	36	76	32	144

$$\chi^2 = 33.04 \text{ ; d.f.} = 4$$
$$P < .01$$

It is not surprising that Table 5.21 shows a highly significant χ^2 value since education, outlook and participation have already appeared as positively interdependent factors. The 'low' participation column shows 5 respondents who have a progressive (high) outlook. They belong to conservative families, who have, however, allowed the respondents to have primary and medium levels of education.

Cultural factors prevent them from taking a more active role in community activity. The same column shows that the number of low level participants increases with a more conservative outlook.

What emerges significantly from the above tables and the χ^2 tests, is that the social participation of respondents is positively related to the respondents' educational level. Both the educational background of the family as well as respondents' own educational level, are important. While it may not be necessary for women to have high levels of education to ensure high social participation, it appears that a certain level of education (even primary only) associated with a family background of education does enable women to participate more effectively in the social life of the rural community. The education that a woman receives builds up her personal confidence and an educated family background helps to remove cultural restrictions on her social participation. Thus the two factors combine to facilitate the process of women's participation in socio-political life.

SUMMARY

A review of the chapter on social participation reveals a significant interdependence between education and participation whereas participation is not so effectively linked with the ascriptive status of respondents.

Most respondents function best at the village level where it is easier to reconcile family responsibility with the requirements of membership. It is this group which shows sparks of political leadership and which needs encouragement and support to grow in the right direction. The group of low-level participants are those whose nominations have been more or less politically motivated. The perception they have of their role in the ZP/PS is, therefore, limited.

Nearly all the respondents would like that more women be present on ZP/PS bodies. They feel more comfortable to participate in the presence of more women. The responses regarding the experience gained during the term of office reveals much that is positive in the way women are growing to face the challenge of a new social role. This response may not be very apparent but it is nonetheless real, as yet small in impact but gaining in confidence and conviction. The respondents evinced the desire for more opportunity to learn, to experience, to widen their horizon of interest. The panchayat structures have provided a few opportunities for this effort but much more remains to be done so that opportunities for self-development may be increased and spread out over the vast numbers of women all over the rural horizon.

6

A COMPARATIVE PROFILE OF WOMEN MEMBERS OF THE ZILLA PARISHADS AND PANCHAYAT SAMITIS IN MAHARASHTRA

INTRODUCTION

Having examined the social background, the developing social outlook and participation of the total sample of respondents, it is opportune at this stage, to view the emergent features that characterise the two populations represented in the sample. They are the ZP women-councillors and the PS members, to whom the same interview schedule was administered.

During the visits to the districts, the researcher tried as far as possible to include ZP representatives who could speak for the district as well as for the block. The sample thus includes 40 ZP women councillors out of a universe of 48, from 24 rural districts of Maharashtra, Nasik having been excluded as explained earlier in Chapter 2. The ZP councillors also being members of the Panchayat Samitis, the total sample covers nearly 50 per cent of women-members at the Block/PS level. For the purpose of drawing a profile of each of the populations, the sample is composed as follows :

	40	women-councillors of Z.P.
	104	women-members of P.S.
Total	144	

The characteristics according to which the profiles of respondents will be drawn are those which describe the ascriptive and achievement status of the members. Ascriptive status includes caste-affiliation, land-holdings, and political influence which characterise the family of the respondent. It has been seen in Chapter 3 that though land-holdings and political influence may be factors of achievement for the husband, they are factors of ascription for the wife who is socially identified with her husband's position in these aspects. Achievement status includes the education, social outlook and social participation of respondents.

The data concerning the above characteristics has already been presented and analysed in its general context in the last three chapters. It will now be distributed according to its incidence among the two populations and the significance of the distributions tested as shown in the following table :

TABLE 6.1 : **A comparative view of respondents at PS/ZP levels**

Variable	Population	Score-Values				χ^2 value	Significance
		1	2	3	4		
1. Caste*	ZP	23	5	6	6	9.06	P < .05
	PS	45	38	14	7	d.f.3	
		H	M	L			
2. Land holdings	ZP	24	9	7		7.05	P < .05
	ZP	55	30	19		d.f.2	
3. Political influence of family	ZP	30	6	4		2.98	P > .05
	PS	62	24	18		d.f.2	
4. Education	ZP	8	22	10		14.07	P < .01
	PS	4	47	53		d.f.2	
5. Social outlook	ZP	21	16	3		5.58	P > .05
	PS	39	41	24		d.f.2	
6. Social participation	ZP	17	19	4		10.79	P < .01
	PS	19	57	28		d.f.2	

*The caste-division as shown in the column "Score-values" is as follows :

1. Brahmin, maratha kshatriya
2. Maratha kunbi, agric. and trading castes
3. Backward classes
4. SC/ST.

The Table 6.1 indicates that there are significant differences in the distributions of the two populations (ZP and PS) with regard to the factors of caste, land-holdings, education and social participation. The first-three items in Table 6.1 describe the ascriptive status of the families from which women-members are chosen. Among these three : Caste, land-holdings and political influence, the variations between the two populations appear mainly in the areas of caste-affiliation and land-holding. The distribution pattern of political influence does not appear to be significantly different.

Items 4, 5 and 6 in Table 6.1 describe the achievement status of respondents and the χ^2 tests show that the two populations have significant differences in the areas of education and social participation but not so in the area of social outlook. The significance of differences between the two populations in the areas of education and social participation is more marked than the differences in caste and land-holdings. This may indicate that the ZP-PS differential among women is more marked by the education-participation differential than that obtaining from ascriptive status. The data contained in Table 6.1 will be further analysed in order to draw a clearer profile of the ZP woman councillor as well as that of the PS representative.

The analysis of both populations will be done in the light of the ascriptive-achievement status of the respondents concerned. The plan for developing the profile is as follows :

(a) Ascriptive Status :
- (i) Caste
- (ii) Land-holdings
- (iii) Political influence

(b) Achievement Status :
- (i) Education
- (ii) Social outlook
- (iii) Social participation.

Ascriptive status

Caste

A caste-wise break-up of the women on the ZP and PS reveals interesting characteristics of the two populations as seen in Table. 6.2.

TABLE 6.2 : **Caste distribution of respondents in the ZP/PS**

Category	Caste/Caste-group	No. of Respondents			
		ZP	%	PS	%
1.	Brahmin	3	7.5	9	8.7
1.	Maratha kshatriya	22	55.0	37	35.5
2.	Maratha kunbi	1	2.5	14	13.4
2.	Agricultural/trading castes	3	7.5	22	21.0
3.	Backward castes	5	12.5	15	14.4
4.	SC/ST	6	15.0	7	7.0
		40	100.0	104	100.0

It is seen from Table 6.2 that the Maratha Kshatriya caste constitutes 55 per cent of the ZP respondents, thus exercising a position of dominance at the district level. In the case of the PS respondents, the Maratha Kshatriya group, while remaining the largest single group, composes only 35 per cent of the sample, and together with the Kunbis, 49 per cent of respondents in the PS.

According to Sirsikar (1970 : 24), politics in Maharashtra is dominated by certain castes, specially the Brahmins, Marathas and Mahars. In the total sample of 144 respondents, it is seen that the Brahmins do not have a numerical superiority as they account for only 8 per cent of the population. Table 1.25 showed them to be politically more powerful than other castes. The Maratha respondents dominate in numbers as well as in land-holding and political influence. The ZP sample of 40 contains a fair percentage of SC/ST groups (15) whereas their percentage is lower (7) in the PS population. Caste-dominance is invested in the Maratha Kshatriya group in the case of ZP women councillors whereas in the case of PS members, the dominance is less clustered and spread more widely over the Intermediate caste-groups.

While caste dominance represents the hold of traditional norms, the widening spectrum of caste-representation is a tribute to the effort of democratic decentralisation which has been initiated through panchayat structures.

Land-holdings

The data in Table 6.3 shows the pattern of land-holding among ZP councillors and PS members as follows :

TABLE 6.3 : **Land-holdings among ZP/PS respondents**

Extent of Land-holding	No. of Respondents			
	ZP	%	PS	%
High	24	60	55	53
Medium	9	22.5	30	29
Low	7	17.5	19	18
Total	40	100.0	104	100

Table 6.3 shows that a larger percentage of ZP councillors come from high land-owning families than in the case of PS members. The χ^2 value shows a significant difference in the distribution pattern. The concentration of a high caste-group among the ZP councillors may also explain the higher concentration of large landowners at that level. The land-owning pattern among the PS members is more diffused among the high and medium groups which can also be explained by the wider distribution of caste-groups. It would appear, therefore, that the traditional symbols of power are more present at the district level than at the block level. Could it be said that there is greater decentralisation of traditionally powerful groups as one moves from the district to the block and village levels ? It would be necessary to study women in gram panchayats to substantiate this trend.

A closer view of the data on land-holdings show that 37.5 per cent of the families at the ZP level and 31 per cent of families at PS level have non-agricultural sources of income. Many of these families have low land-holdings, and one-third of these belong to backward and SC/ST caste groups. What is important by way of observation is that people with non-agricultural occupation are also able to have political influence and to be selected on these bodies. Low land-holdings in a traditional rural society would mean a lower economic status, but viewed with professional competence, service occupation or business enterprise, this factor projects a different pattern of status. But high landowners and low landholders have additional non-agricultural sources of income. For the former their economic status is thus enhanced and they become proportionately influential. For the latter these sources provide an opportunity to rise in economic status and establish wider social contacts which enable them to compete on more or less equal terms with the traditionally big landowners.

Going back to the data analysed it is seen that the ZP woman-councillor generally comes from a high land-owning family. At the PS level the member also generally belongs to a family having large holdings but here there are greater chances of representation even from among families with lower land-holdings. Thus, while it is seen that, to a large extent, the traditional power of land-holdings still determines a major portion of representation at the ZP and PS levels, the panchayat structure offers scope also for non-traditional symbols of economic status. Will this wider option offered by 'panchayati raj' mean increased representation for those whose economic status is based on assets other than land-holdings as for instance the SC/ST classes who are generally known, to be marginal farmers or landless labourers ? This question is answered to some extent in Table 3.21 which shows that out of the 14 respondents appearing in "low" caste, 7 are medium and 5 low land-holders, but the husbands have economic status by professional practice or commercial units. In these latter, cases it seems as if economic sufficiency more than caste is a qualifying factor and if so, the question of involving economically marginal groups in the system still poses a challenge.

Political influence

Table 6.1 shows that there is no significant difference in the pattern of distribution of political influence between the ZP and PS populations.

The data indicates that the large majority of respondents fall in the 'high' category. At the ZP level, the cushion of high political influence is more marked since 75 per cent of the respondents belong to this category as against 60 per cent at the PS level.

Another interesting feature of ZP women councillors is that 18 out of the 40 representatives, live most of the time in taluka or district headquarters. Seventeen of these families are in the category of high political influence. Thus 45 per cent of ZP respondents are fairly close to or actual residents of urban centres.

Migration towards urban centres is a growing trend. People who desire to climb the ladder of socio-political power look forward to having an additional establishment in the district headquarters or in a bigger city where wider social contacts can be made. It also ensures social prominence for the wives of the politically active leaders who may aspire to be nominated on panchayat bodies irrespective of their being true representatives of women at the rural grass-roots.

One may say of the political profile of the ZP and PS representative that she comes from a family with high political involvement.

Achievement status

Education

A comparative view of the levels of education at the ZP and PS levels, reveals some significant differences as shown in Table 6.4 :

TABLE 6.4 : **Educational levels of members of the ZP/PS**

Educational Level	No. of Respondents			
	ZP	%	PS	%
1. High	8	20	4	4
2. Middle	22	55	47	45
3. Low	10	25	53	51
Total	40	100	104	100

The most striking point of difference is that the majority group of ZP councillors have a middle-school level of education whereas the majority of PS members are at the low or below primary level of education. Of the 12 post S.S.C. respondents in the total sample, 8 are found in the ZP. Ten of them are the wives of big landowners and 2 of husbands who are low landholders but practising lawyers. Most of them also come from homes where the husband has one or more non-agricultural source of income, which again means better economic status and a fair amount of contact with urban centres.

Since it is seen that there is a high degree of correlation between the educational level of the husband and that of the wife (Table 3.23) could one say that the significance of differences reflected among the women-members at the educational level would also be reflected among their husbands in the two populations . The following Table 6.5 gives a comparative view of the significance of educational levels of the respondents and their husbands :

TABLE 6.5 : **A Comparative view of the educational levels of respondents and husbands**

		Educational Levels			χ^2 Value	Significance	γ
		H	M	L			
Respondents	ZP	8	22	10	14.07	$P < .01$	.53
	PS	4	47	53	d.f.2		
Husbands	ZP	12	21	7	8.91	$P < .05$	.37
	PS	11	65	27	d.f.2		

Table 6.5 shows that the differences in the educational levels of husbands of respondents at ZP/PS levels is less marked than in the case of the respondents in the two populations. This may help to indicate that while there is correlation between the husband's and wife's level of education her achievement in this area is not merely a question of following suit with the husband but an achievement which depends on other factors, of which her own interest and ability may be an important consideration.

Social outlook

Table 6.1 shows that there is no significant difference in the distribution pattern of ZP and PS representatives. The general movement shows signs of shedding conservatism in favour of progressivism. The differences seen in the educational levels of respondents in the two populations do not feature markedly in their social outlook. As already mentioned in Chapter 4, there are other factors besides education that may influence the social outlook of respondents. In the case of ZP respondents, the majority are in the 'higher progressive' group whereas in the case of the PS representatives, the majority are in the 'moderate' group.

Social participation

The participation of women at the ZP and PS levels is seen to be significantly different in Table 6.1. ZP woman councillors belong mostly to the medium and high levels of participation whereas PS members participate at the medium and low levels.

Since it has been established (Table 5.19) that education and participation are significantly co-related it may be said that a higher level of education at the ZP level also brings in its wake a higher level of participation.

What may be the reason for a marked association between education and participation ? Participation involves confrontation with society and in the context of the panchayat structure it calls for dealing with officials, non-officials, people of all castes and classes. Above all, in a male-dominated set-up where traditional bindings still restrict the social orbit of the rural woman, her participation calls for considerable self-confidence to face the challenges in the public sphere. To be in the know of panchayat activity, literacy helps because of certain procedures in its functioning. While it is true that knowledge of the 3 R's does not by itself mould leaders, and there are examples even in this study to illustrate the point, yet it has to be conceded that those who occupy formal positions of leadership are able to function better when they can read and write as well. Today, especially among elite classes in rural areas, education is considered to be a social asset, and a general norm of progress. The researcher, in her personal interviews with respondents, was able to feel the self-confidence of women who had some opportunity of formal education against the embarrassment of women who felt inhibited to reply that they had not been to school or that they had studied only up to the primary level. To have education has become a matter of pride even if the respondent's social performance may not measure up to her level of formal education.

Women both on the PS and ZP have fairly high scores in participation levels. This reflects their potential which awaits recognition, in order to express itself more fully.

A summary of the main observations regarding the ascriptive and achievement status of women functioning in ZP and PS bodies of Maharashtra may be illustrated as follows :

TABLE 6.6 : **Profiles of women representatives on ZP and PS bodies**

The ZP Councillor is generally of :	The P.S. Member is generally of :
1. the Maratha kshatriya caste	1. the Maratha/other Intermediate castes.
2. a family with high land-holdings	2. a family with high and medium size land-holdings.
3. a family with high political influence	3. a family with high political influence.

TABLE 6.6 —*contd.*

The ZP Councillor is generally of :	The P.S. Member is generally of :
She has :	She has :
4. an education above Std. VII	4. an education up to Std. IV.
5. a highly progressive outlook on social issues concerning women	5. a moderately progressive outlook on social issues concerning women.
6. a high and medium level of social participation	6. a low and medium level of social participation.

In Table 6.6 which depicts the findings regarding the ascriptive and achievement status of ZP and PS representatives it may be observed that the selection of ZP and PS representatives appears to be made on the basis of considerations like caste, land-holdings and political influence of the family. At the ZP level, these factors are more pronounced. What is true of leadership among men is also more or less true of the existing leadership among women as their suitability for selection on panchayat bodies is measured by family status and influence. "Studies on panchayati raj leadership reveal that caste and landownership are the dominant factors which determine the position and status of leaders at the local level. (Chandiramani ; 1979 : 187)

There are changes that are being effected by the spread of higher education and the expansion of professional service as well as varied forms of non-agricultural occupation. Such changes also influence the rural family and thereby the status, outlook and participation of women. The sample shows that several have taken up residence in more important centres of the district, increasing the radius of their influence by participation in various socio-political activities. While such growth can be termed as progress especially from the standpoint of formal education and social participation such as envisaged in this study, it is the impact of this development on women at the grass-root levels of rural society that is the major concern. Is the development that is observed at ZP and PS levels merely helping to project the image of a few influential women or is it helping to build leaders who can truly represent the vast masses of rural women ? This is a question that derives from the much broader perspective of political leadership in the country at large.

It is to be noted from the data that in spite of similarities in ascriptive status, the performance of women in terms of social participation tends to show some differences in involvement at the district and block levels. Education which stands out as an important variable, reinforces the personal potential of women and strengthens her ability to take action for the community. What about other variables which may influence participation, such as family support, extent of family responsibility, location of residence. These factors have surfaced but they have not been a special focus of study as is the case for education. It would be worthwhile studying in greater depth the impact of all these variables on the social participation of women in order to see how leadership among women can find more effective expression at the district, block and village levels.

7

CONCLUSION

The present study set itself to find out the socio-economic background of women-members on the Zilla Parishads and Panchayat Samitis of Maharashtra and the factors that helped or hindered them in the performance of their roles as members. Indirectly it was hoped that the above findings would throw light on the situation regarding the contribution of women who were statutorily present on these bodies. The study aimed at achieving an understanding of the present situation within the context of past influences as well as the process of social change which is orienting women's response for the future. The underlying motivation was to discover the potential of women in rural areas and how far they are able to give expression to it in present organisational structures for development, the most important one of which being Panchayati Raj for rural India.

The sample chosen for the study consists of 144 women-members of the ZP and PS in 24 districts of Maharashtra. The sample covers nearly 50 per cent of the universe. The interviews were conducted personally by the researcher either in the homes of the respondents or in the ZP or PS offices in the district.

Social-economic background of respondents

Caste

The majority of respondents belong to the dominant caste of Maratha Kshatriyas and Maratha Kunbis who constitute 51 per cent of the sample though their percentage in the population of Maharashtra is estimated at 40 per cent (Sirsikar; 1970 : 40). The intermediate castes which include the land-owning (excluding the Kunbis) and trading castes, account for 17 per cent of the sample. They enjoy economic and numerical superiority as compared with the Brahmins who have high ritual status but are about 6 per cent in the general population of Maharashtra (Karve; 1968 : 76) and 8 per cent in the sample. The SC/ST are under-represented in the sample where they number 7.63 per cent whereas they constitute 12 per cent of the total population in Maharashtra (Census 1971).

The Pune and Marathwada Divisions have the highest concentration of the Maratha Kshatriya caste-group. Though there is domination by this particular caste-group it is encouraging to observe that the panchayat structure has effectively mobilised women of backward and SC/ST caste-groups to also hold position on these bodies. The fact that a woman from the 'Mahar' caste can sit beside a member of the Maratha Kshatriya caste and even share a cup of tea, is a significant development in a traditional caste-bound rural society. The sample also contains several members of non-Maharashtrian origin who have so identified themselves with the local population and won their confidence as to be co-opted on the local panchayat bodies. Thus the process of democratic decentralization has been set in motion; slow though the movement may be, sure is the hope that it will lay the foundation of a healthy democratic tradition in rural society.

Land-holdings

Nearly 50 per cent of respondents come from families who claim having about 20 acres of land or even more. Taking the average size of ownership-holding in Maharashtra as 9.42 acres (NSS ; 1960-61 : 3), 101 respondents which is 70 per cent of the sample, thus have ownership holdings much above the average. The significant χ^2 value between land-holdings and caste shows that the numerically superior Maratha caste enjoys a position of dominance with regard to land-holdings as well. Many of these families once enjoyed traditional positions of authority in the village, such as those of "patil" and "deshmukh".

There is an over-representation of the high landowning class who form a small percentage of the population as compared with the poor representation of low land-holders (0-5 acres) who constitute the bulk of the rural population. The backward and SC/ST caste-groups have land-holdings as follows : 7 in the high land-holding category 15 with medium size land-holdings and 11 low land-holders. The SC/ST respondents from the high and medium land-holding categories have come to represent the elite among their caste groups.

Though land-holding is an important source of power in the rural community, yet the sample contains a number of members who belong to families with marginal land-holdings. Out of a total of 144 families in the sample, 79 have over 15 acres of land; 39 between 5 and 15 acres and 26 have less than 5 acres of land. Today, land-holdings do not constitute the only source of income for the rural household. Forty-seven families, constituting 33 per cent of the sample, have non-agricultural sources of income by way of professional or service occupation, or business enterprise. The high-caste and high land owning group tends to go for professional occupation (lawyers especially) and for business enterprise. The low land-holders who are very heterogeneous in caste-structure go in mainly for service occupation and small business enterprise. For the high land-owning group, additional income from non-agricultural sources indicates affluence. The majority of such families enjoy a fairly high extent of economic sufficiency, and also wider contacts with urban areas. Twenty respondents maintained two establishments : one in the city/taluka centre where the children pursued their education and the husband maintained social, political, professional or business contacts, and the other in the hereditary village where older family members looked after the family property.

Those with low land-holdings who could count in a limited way on the yield of the property also preferred to have a regular source of income through non-agricultural occupation. They maintain regular touch with urban areas because of the influential contacts it permits.

Educational background of family

The education of the parents of the respondents shows the wide gap that existed between male and female literacy over thirty years ago, the ratio of percentages in the sample being 76 : 28. The figures are however much higher than the ratio of percentages existing in the 1951 Census (p.141) for male and female literacy which is 25.98 : 6.54. It appears from the same census that literacy is related to socio-economic status, so that a higher level of education is generally indicative of a higher socio-economic status.

The Maratha Kshatriya and Kunbi caste-groups constituted a

"rural aristocracy" in terms of land-holdings but they remained "largely illiterate". (Karve; 1968 : 76). Their over-protective attitude towards women in the practice of purdah and not sending her for education resulted in keeping female education at a low level. Thus today, socio-economic positions of power to which these castes have risen assure their women of being selected on political bodies like the ZP/PS but the performance of these women is handicapped by the lack of a background of education.

However, the process of social change is gradually affecting the traditional high landowning families and their economic security permits them to benefit from expanding opportunities in the field of education. Whereas the majority of fathers of respondents belonged to the illiterate or primary education category, the majority of husbands of the respondents have studied between Std. VII and the S.S.C. The number of graduates, post-graduates as well as professionally educated husbands is considerably higher than in the case of the fathers. These factors have influenced the education of women because educated fathers are more disposed to educate their daughters and educated husbands want to have educated wives. The gamma correlation test shows a high positive relation between the father's education and that of the daughter (.72) as well as between the husband's and wife's level of education (.80). The higher percentage of literacy and education among the respondents as compared with their mothers may be attributed largely to parental influence (father's particularly) as also to other factors of social change like the expansion of educational opportunities in rural areas.

Political background

The socio-political background of the parental home of the respondents shows that 33 respondents recalled the involvement of their fathers, brothers, mothers, uncles and other relatives in various forms of socio-political activity, the most outstanding of which was the freedom movement. The respondents attributed specially to their fathers their own interest in socio-political activity. Again it is of interest to note that 3 mothers of respondent and a sister were involved in the independence movement, having braved imprisonment more than once during this period.

With regard to the socio-political background of the husband's home, 110 respondents (or 76 per cent of the sample) had one or more members of their husband's family engaged in socio-political activity. In most cases it was the husband who was so engaged. As compared with the spontaneous involvement of mothers and sisters in the freedom-movement, the present involvement of respondents in panchayat bodies has a more formal aspect given the changed socio-political context of the country. Though the statutory clause regarding women's representation asks for women's participation in a new form, it continues the spirit of the independence movement, involving women politically as well as in the social task of development.

The husbands are generally involved in political activity of which, membership in panchayat bodies is a part. It is felt that their association with welfare organisations or agricultural/marketing co-operatives is usually a result of their political influence and a means to increase the scope of that influence in the rural community. A quantitative assessment of the husband's political influence shows that 64 per cent of the respondents come from families with high political influence, 21 per cent have a medium degree of influence and 15 per cent have very low or no political influence at all. The overwhelming presence of respondents belonging to families having a high and medium degree of political influence indicates the importance of this consideration in the choice of women-candidates for nomination to ZP/PS bodies. The presence of the 15 per cent of non-influential candidates indicates that the panchayat structure also stands by criteria other than political influence. Among these are respondents whose innate leadership qualities among the women of the local community have been recognised.

The political influence of the husband is significantly related to caste as well as to land-holdings which indicates that traditional symbols of authority still wield considerable influence in the political career of rural leaders. However, education which is making increasing headway among this traditionally influential group introduces several elements of change :

(a) it is helping the traditionally powerful group to become more powerful.

(b) it is helping non-traditionally powerful groups to become more powerful since it is also accessible to them.

(c) it has become a *sine qua non* for organisational involvement and as such its power over-shadows the social position of caste and possession of land.

One may, therefore, say that education serves as an equalising factor among various caste-groups and economic classes. The power that education can exercise to promote social equality will depend on its accessibility to all classes of society. The analysis of Table 3.25 shows that there is more equalisation of caste-groups in the sample on the educational front than on other factors. In this regard one may say that the effort to promote universal education should be strengthened much more, specially for socially and economically weaker sections.

Personal Background of Respondents

Age

The mean age of respondents is 45 years which shows the presence of an older range of women on ZP/PS bodies. The general tendency in rural areas has been to choose leaders, senior in age. The sample consists of a majority of women who have been married before the age of 16 years and who are relatively free from family responsibility by the age of 45 because their children are grown-up or settled and many have daughters-in-law to attend to domestic responsibilities as the situation demands. The position of 'mother' or 'mother-in-law' promotes the woman in the rural family to a position of authority and respect. Seniority in age also wins more acceptance for her in the larger circle of the rural community.

At the same time, there are signs of change in the traditional age-pattern of leaders. Twenty-eight per cent of the sample consists of women between the ages of 26 and 37 years, who have had some formal education. They have youth and education on their side, and can enliven as also give direction to group participation. Generally caught up with family responsibilities specially that of having small children to care for, they attend the ZP/PS meetings once a month or once in 3 months but they cannot be free to participate frequently in the social activities of the community, as is possible in the case of older women.

Marital status

All but one of the respondents were married as is expected of women in the rural community; 28 respondents (19 per cent of the sample) were widows ; 2 were separated and among the married women, 7 had a co-wife status.

It is interesting to note that women who might have been relegated to a position of inferiority or social ostracism in traditional society, as was the case with widows or women separated in marriage, have been recognised as members of ZP/PS bodies. Modern organisational structures like the panchayat set-up being based on the new values of democracy and respect for the individual go a long way in exercising a healthy influence on the trend of women's development despite resistance to change usually found in rural society.

Number of children

The average number of children born by respondents is 3. Quite a number of respondents are childless—15 per cent of the sample. A childless woman was not looked upon with favour in the traditional rural community, but this outlook shows evident signs of change.

It is interesting to link the common findings regarding the marital status and number of children among the respondents. The majority of respondents are at an age when the burden of family responsibility is lighter ; 28 respondents are widows who are generally over 50 years ; 22 respondents have no children ; 7 are co-wives. These observations point to the fact that women who have less family responsibilities more easily accept the choice of being on ZP/PS bodies.

Education

It has been seen already that the educational progress of respondents has been largely influenced by the parental home, especially the father. The percentage sex differential in literacy rates between the fathers and mothers of respondents (76 : 29) is considerably reduced in the present sample as shown in the percentage ratio of literacy between husbands and the respondents which is 94 : 84. Over 50 per cent of the respondents have studied up to the VII Std. and 25 per cent have studied up to the S.S.C. and degree courses. The relative progress in literacy rates made by women as compared with that of men, shows important strides and thus raises hope for the future.

Eight respondents had taken various courses of professional training : in teaching, nursing and homeopathy. Five respondents had taken up employment for a certain period of time : three as teachers, one as a nurse ; one respondent participated in radio programmes; another worked for an Adivasi Trust. The respondent who was unmarried, had worked as a headmistress for almost 40 years ; three of those who took up employment had contracted marriage of their own choice and were obliged to support themselves during the early period of marriage. One respondent had worked as a gram sevika for a short period of time. Most of those who went for higher education were motivated to do so by their husbands.

The above flashes on a few respondents are significant in that they point to a process of change which is being effected in the motivation and life-styles of women in rural areas. They are not significant in terms of numbers but as indicators of an emerging trend which will increase with the expansion of educational and work opportunities in a developing economy. These opportunities affect not only the location of operation but cultural practices, patterns of thought and behaviour which will be gradually reflected in the quality of women's participation on panchayat bodies.

Some of the cases cited as examples of women's leadership (Chapter 3) highlight the role of education in enabling women steeped in the conservative practices of traditional society to play a dynamic role in helping local women to find opportunities for their development and to attend to basic needs in the community.

The socio-economic background of respondents shows both, the presence of the traditional as well as the signs of a social change that cannot be stemmed in a developing country. The caste factor is still strong and influences cultural practice as well as the course of political power. Education emerges as an important force behind the social change that is taking place in rural society. It is used on the one hand to consolidate the power of traditional strongholds and on the other its accessibility as well as its "indispensability" makes it a potent factor in the hands of the traditionally weaker sections of society. In the case of men, education has become a source of economic and political gain. In the case of rural women, education has become an instrument of social liberation. The rural social strata among which education is spreading rapidly is a privileged sector as the present sample of respondents shows. Economic gain is, therefore, not envisaged in the case of these women. The gain for them is social and cultural. The panchayat statute has opened the way for women's representation ; education enhances the way for women's social contribution. The path has been blazed through the education of the father and the husband. Gradually the influence of the mother's education will be felt increasingly. This collaboration on the part of the family is absolutely necessary for the movement of women's participation to continue and for the results to be effective. The process of social change that is occurring in rural society manifests an admirable blending of the 'ancient' and the 'new'.

Social outlook and awareness

This section aimed at discovering :

(a) the thought pattern and awareness of respondents on social issues, problems and services affecting the welfare of women in rural areas, and
(b) the ability of women to express themselves on these issues.

The answers given by respondents show first of all that women do think about these issues and that they are able to express an opinion about them. Thus the myth of having mere "ho mannarbais" or "yes" women on these bodies has no credence. What is of importance to note is that women do have opinions to contribute in the deliberations of ZP/PS meetings and that they need to develop confidence to give expression to their thought in such public bodies. It is also important for those who conduct such meetings to note that silence on the part of women need not be equated with ignorance. On several occasions, the researcher was discouraged from going all out to meet the P.S. members who hardly opened their mouths at meetings. Reading the minds of the officials they seemed to say : "Coming all the way from Bombay, just to meet these 'dumb' women." At the end of the interview, accompanying staff-members often showed surprise with a flavour of admiration at seeing these women acquit themselves so creditably in answering the researcher. The women themselves were happy to find that they were able to satisfy the researcher as many were nervous at the start of the interview. Soon after the interview some of them proudly remarked to those around : "She asked us lots of information and we gave it". One respondent (Dhobi by caste) who had arrived well in advance of the time fixed for the interview said that her husband had asked her not to serve him his meal, but to go in time to meet the 'bai' from Bombay. "I thought, who will come from Bombay to see me", she expressed in all simplicity. Several respondents asked the researcher : "Now that you have asked all these questions and we have replied, what will you do with it ?

After almost every interview, the respondent or someone in the family asked the researcher to give them her Bombay address. The above observations only help to illustrate that rural women though diffident to express themselves in public bodies are becoming more aware of the social reality around them and are eager to be more involved in the social life of the community. This desire to know and participate is undoubtedly developing and needs to be channelised in order to be effective.

With regard to areas where national policy has given a clear indication : removal of caste discrimination, universal compulsory education, higher age at marriage, abolition of dowry, encouraging the small family norm, the majority of women were fully in accord and may be termed to that extent, progressive.

With regard to socio-cultural practices like co-education, self-choice in marriage, equal partnership with the husband in marriage, participation in social activity outside the house, religious observance, the views expressed reflected a mature assessment of situations, some more traditionally inclined, some oriented towards change, but with a sound core of 'common sense' animating their particular views. It is important to grasp the socio-economic context in which cultural practices take shape. At times it appears as if social legislation is ineffective because of 'unenlightened attitudes' in rural areas but the 'deviants' may be more enlightened in their rural socio-economic context than the urban-inspired legislators. An example of this is the reaction to raising the age of marriage in rural areas.

Marriage and the family have great value for the rural woman. The husband, the children and the home are priority areas which may not be sacrificed for anything else. Her duties towards the husband are always assured and she would never accept a social commitment like that of membership on ZP/PS bodies unless the husband wanted it, irrespective even of the views of in-laws on this issue. Most women agreed that women should participate in social activity (e.g. Mahila Mandals) outside the home and even take up a job if that was possible, but not at the cost of the home and family-life, except where economic necessity may leave no choice in the matter. Even regarding widows, the general opinion favoured remarriage, only if she had no children. If she did have children, it was felt that the woman should live for her children and not jeopardise their happiness by another marriage.

On the whole, the respondents fare better in their answers on outlook rather than on awareness which touches on more factual data. The awareness of women regarding problems, needs and services in the areas of education, health and employment was seen to be high among a few of the educated, politically influential, more urbanised respondents. However most of them found it difficult to answer specific questions regarding services and their availability e.g. balwadis, health-centres, employment projects, agro-industries in their areas. Many respondents had hardly given a thought to these needs since the problems exist more at the level of the underprivileged sectors. Cultural practices do not encourage this class of women to mingle freely outside the home, so that the circle of their contacts tends to remain restricted to their own caste and social class. In spite of these limitations, many respondents argued in favour of removing the socio-economic handicaps of the poorer sections of the rural population. It is in this area that greater awareness needs to be stimulated in any training course for panchayat representatives. This is also the reason why representation needs to be expanded to cover a wider range of socio-economic groups.

The data show that respondents have some idea of the social problems around them, which it is hoped may soon develop into a deeper understanding of the problem and possible action required in the field.

Social participation

General observation

Social participation or action on the part of ZP/PS members is the touchstone of their success as members. The participation of women members has been quantitatively assessed on the basis of certain measurable criteria, as contained in the data. The majority of 53 per cent are "medium" level participant, 25 per cent are in the "high" category and 22 per cent score in the "low" category. Many of the high performers are found to be close to urban areas and they belong to families with agricultural as well as non-agricultural sources of income. Several of the husbands of these respondents are lawyers, with an establishment in the taluka or district centre. The medium and low level participants operate mostly in the village setting. They are good examples of women's leadership in the closeness of villages, easily identifying with and mobilising those around them.

Among the type of assistance that women are able to render through the ZP/PS, activities for women (Mahila Mandals and the education of the children balwadi) seem to be the most commonly undertaken ones. This observation accords with the role expected of women-members as mentioned in the Report of the Committee on Panchayati Raj (1978 : 140-141). Women-members also reported involvement in procuring basic amenities like drinking water taps, wells, construction of approach roads for their villages ; obtaining agricultural inputs for farmers; finding employment opportunities or financial aid for various categories of people in need. How far and how fast can the panchayat structure help women to be yet more effective as members representing and responding to the needs of their local communities should be the major concern for the future.

A fuller participation on the part of women-members, calls for adjustment to a new social role : such as movement outside one's home, sitting at meetings with men, expressing themselves in public, being able to reconcile to the uncertainty of public transport, etc. For younger women, such adjustment is more difficult to effect. In the case of those who go to work for their daily bread, calling for participation may mean exposure to economic insecurity. The new social role is a challenge to women of all strata as well as to their milieu to accept change and adopt practical steps to facilitate a broad-based participation.

Participation and education

The participation of women was found to be significantly linked with education at three levels : the respondents' own educational level, that of her husband and that of her general family background. Even though members belonged to high-caste, high land-owning or highly politically involved families, their participation was generally found to be low in the case of illiterate respondents or those who had just a couple of years in the primary school. There were on the other hand respondents who did not enjoy a high socio-economic status but a low level of primary education was enough to awaken the potential of leadership in them. The data contains some fine examples of leadership among all strata of rural women (Ch. 3 and 4).

While education does appear as an important intervening variable for participation, it cannot be concluded that education and participation are so absolutely related that a high level of participation would necessarily indicate a high level of education. The data show that women with primary and below primary education have also shown good leadership potential. This means that while a certain extent of education is important to develop confidence for social participation, there would be other factors which also enable women to participate actively in public life. The researcher observed that personal ability, family support and tradition were other variables that exercise varying shades of influence. The data definitely show that the general educational background of the respondent as reflected in the father's and husband's levels of education was significantly related with her own educational performance as well as her level of social participation.

It has also been seen in the section on socio-economic background, that the age of the respondent is an important factor in the participation of women. Older women are more free from household responsibilities and their public appearance in rural society is better accepted.

Training for participation

It was observed that 80 respondents had already had some experience of membership in panchayat bodies. Sixty-two women had been in gram panchayats for a period ranging from 5 to 10 years, 34 in panchayat samitis and 14 in zilla parishads. Eleven respondents had held positions in these bodies at different times in the capacity of sarpanch, upsarpanch and upsabhapati. One respondent had the unique honour of being the only woman to occupy the position of chairman of the zilla parishad. It is evident from the data that the women who are selected on these bodies move in circles where the reins of power may be pulled in favour of their co-option not only once but for consecutive terms of office.

The fact that co-option gives a woman all the powers of an elected member makes political parties want to use the possibility of this kind of membership to the maximum. They prefer not to have elected women because the election of a woman closes the door to the possibility of co-option and thereby deprives them of an additional vote. Generally speaking, men are elected and women are co-opted, thus keeping to the letter of the statute regarding women's representation on these bodies. The researcher found that only 6 women had come to be represented on the ZP by election,

Women-candidates are not encouraged to stand for election, even though they may have the capacity to do so.

Again, the researcher felt that women would appreciate some training or orientation in the performance of their role as members. The majority of respondents have not had such opportunity as shown by their attendance at camps/training courses. It is mostly their family background influence as well as a certain lived experience during the period of membership, which help to steer them through. It is also important to have these camps close to their villages.

Contacts with SC/ST

A very broad investigation into the area of women-members' contacts with SC/ST leads to some general observations which could be further explored :

(i) There is a wide gap in the socio-economic levels of the respondents and the SC/ST groups that constitute a large section of the rural population.

(ii) A certain resentment was expressed against the 'excessive' reservation of concessions in education without assuring any follow-up as to the actual use that was made by the SC/ST group.

(iii) Contacts are generally made on the occasion of implementation of social welfare programmes, as also during elections.

(iv) The activity of the Social Welfare Committee of the ZP has helped to promote greater interest for the problems and needs of SC/ST among women representatives.

(v) Social contacts with SC/ST women of a more informal nature are evident on the occasion of a national celebration, a wedding in the house of a land-owner in whose employment they may be or a religious-cultural festival like Sharada Utsav, Satya-Narayan Puja, Ambedkar Jayanti.

The contacts with SC/ST groups have been furthered mainly by the democratic procedure of elections in the political system adopted by the country. Despite certain abuses that creep into these procedures, there cannot but be the recognition of mutual need—the voters for favours for themselves and those seeking election for the support of the voters. Actually election campaigns, have helped to cut across caste and sex barriers.

Participation of social background

The social background factors affecting the selection and participation of respondents, may be illustrated by the Fig. 7.1.

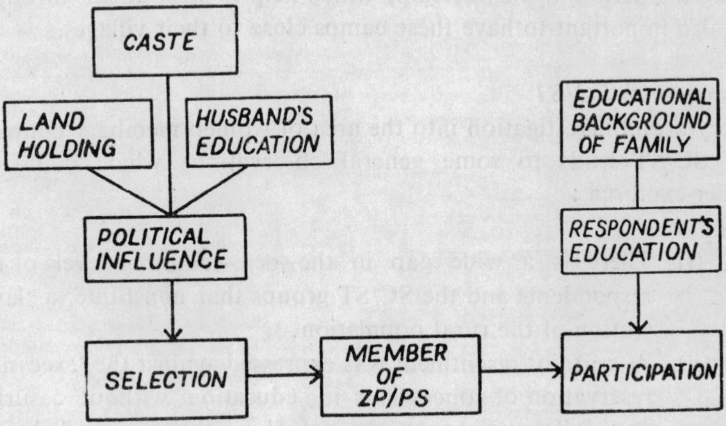

FIG. 7.1 : *Factors Affecting Selection and Participation of Respondents*

Fig 7.1. highlights the important factors affecting the selection and the participation of women-members of ZP/PS. It centres on two important points of membership among women-members :

(1) Selection or the opportunity to participate
(2) Participation or the utilisation of the opportunity.

Selection

The data has shown that 85 per cent of the husbands of respondents are politically involved, 64 per cent at a high level, 21 per cent at a medium level. While there is a small percentage of 15 which has low political involvement and a few none at all, it cannot be denied that the overwhelming majority of women come into prominence at these levels because of the political position of their husbands or other family members. It has already been seen in the section on socio-economic background of respondents that the political status of the husband is positively co-related with caste, land-holding and educational status. All these constitute ascriptive factors as far as the social position of the woman is concerned. *Her selection on ZP/PS bodies is, therefore, at present largely a matter of ascription.*

One may say that the factor of the husband's education which enters into the game of political influence, has an important role to play in that educated husbands permit their wives to appear in the social role expected of them as members of ZP/PS bodies. Some permit them to merely attend meetings and sign a register ; others encourage a more active role. However, taking the very appearance of the woman on the panchayat body as a step forward in her social participation, one may recognise in it a break with tradition and a promising opportunity for women to make their contribution to social development at par with men.

Participation

It has already been pointed out that in the matter of active social involvement of the respondent in ZP/PS activities, the ascriptive factors of caste, land-holdings and political influence do not have as important an influence as the educational factor. Women's ability to participate actively is influenced by her own educational level and the educational status of the family : parental as well as that of her husband. *Participation among women on ZP/PS bodies is thus seen to be considerably influenced by her achievement status, specially in the area of education.* There are several cases ...d in the analysis (Ch. 4) which show that the element of personal ...ity is unmistakably present so much so that even a low level of education is enough to draw out the leadership potential. Ascriptive factors are important in so far as they make education more accessible to the respondent as compared with women of the socially and economically underprivileged sectors. Education being a right of every citizen, women of all sectors should be able to avail themselves of educational facilities and thus prepare themselves for effective participation on panchayat bodies.

Perception of membership role

With regard to women's perception of their own role as members of the ZP/PS, most members felt that they had gained in knowledge and experience by having been present regularly at ZP/PS meetings. Most had little or no idea of their function since they had been co-opted without any orientation as to the role expected of them. As long as they attended meetings and signed the attendance register, both the women and those who sponsored them were satisfied. While they did express interest in the discussions at the meetings they remained for the most part, passive spectators, especially in the initial period of their membership.

Many respondents were ready to be members for yet another term in case it was thus decided by the family. For many of these the membership position enhances the social status of the family even when their actual involvement in the body remains at its lowest. The respondents would have liked to be more enlightened about their role on ZP/PS but apparently such opportunities of information hardly existed. Most active respondents had had the required orientation in their own family backgrounds. For instance in the case of respondents whose parents or close relatives had been freedom-fighters or who had been in government service, specially at the ministerial level, their motivation for involvement in social service or political organisations was reflected strongly. The influence of the family on the participation of respondents is very great. A few respondents might have wanted to be more socially involved but socio-cultural restrictions at home obliged them to restrain their interest.

Women-members agreed unanimously that seats should be reserved for them. Most members suggested that the number of seats be increased because it was somewhat awkward for them to sit sometimes alone amidst so many men and be expected to take active part. Among the more educated and progressive participants, the number of women members did not matter as much as the capacity or ability of the women chosen to speak and act effectively as required.

EMERGENT ISSUES AND SUGGESTIONS

The position of the elite in panchayati raj

The study shows that women of the upper castes, wives of big landowners and politically influential families tend to dominate the positions reserved for women in the ZP/PS of Maharashtra. This situation cannot be helped to a great extent because traditional structures tend to perpetuate themselves. Moreover these traditionally privileged castes are economically better placed to use the new opportunities of development in the process of social change. Thus the elite among them can acquire new sources of power (as seen in the case of professionals) and so entrench themselves firmly in positions of dominance and influence.

The above observations give rise to a spate of questions: How can women who enter the structure of panchayati raj because of their protected ascriptive status, really contribute towards the development of rural society, specially the weaker sections ? Given their backgrounds, are they conversant enough with the problems faced by the disadvantaged sectors or would they naturally prefer to defend their own interests behind walls of tradition ? Does the milieu in which the majority of these women live open them to a broader view of the needs of rural society ?

While one has to recognize the existing position of dominance by the traditionally elite classes exercised within a limited perspective, one cannot fail to also see the breaks that are being effected in the traditional structure through organisations like panchayati raj. The democratic nature of these institutions has widened the sources which invest people with socio-political status. In addition to hereditary position or notwithstanding it, there are factors like education, economic status, leadership ability which also determine the political standing of individuals. Often it is a combination of the above factors which give individuals sufficient political clout to steer their way into these bodies. That education, economic status, leadership ability can compete with hereditary positions indicate greater possibilities of a rise to power on the strength of achievement factors. This raises the green signal for those whose ritual status has traditionally confined them to positions of subservience. Thus one may say that panchayati raj provides broader opportunities of social representation. While its present composition is certainly not the last word in democratic decentralization, it is heartening to note the setting off of a movement in that direction.

At present, women are more bound by ascriptive factors than men, but the social change which gives greater importance to achievement and which is influencing the wider social context is bound to effect the mentality and functioning of women as well. The study has definitely highlighted admirable examples of leadership among women : of high and low caste, affluent and poorer, of Maharashtrian origin or domiciled settlers, educated and illiterate, young and old, widow or co-wife. These examples may not be numerous but that they have manifested themselves in rural society and found recognition on panchayat bodies is evidence of a change that has been initiated.

In what way is this newly emergent type of leadership on panchayat bodies elitist ? One could say that it is mainly on the ground of economic status. All have economic sufficiency, many are in situations of affluence some by ascription, others by achievement. The common denominator among the elite in panchayati raj today is economic sufficiency, allied with political influence.

Economic power has become the great dividing line between the few who possess and the masses who live below poverty line. How far are the 'elite' women-members truly representative of the cause of economically and socially weaker sections of rural women ? Are they able to voice the needs of these sectors who should be the first beneficiaries of development programmes ? The study shows instances of women who have been active in enabling weaker sections to benefit from panchayat programmes of aid. Many are active in the local circles in which they feel familiar. The outlook and participation pattern of women-members shows a readiness to change and adapt but their pace of progress is largely measured by the positive or negative influence of their surroundings. In short, women reflect the in-built attitudes that characterise their milieu and given the strong traditionalism of rural society, their attitudes tend to be more set. However, there is enough evidence in the study to show that given the right type of orientation and opportunity to contribute, women, whether of the elite or less privileged class, can be encouraged to play a more meaningful role in panchayati raj.

Need of wider representation

Recognising that dominance by any caste or class tends to uphold the interests of that particular group to the detriment of wider social interests it may be better to increase the number of seats for women so as to open the chances of a wider representation. How this may be done so as to avoid the prevalent pattern of dominance, is a question for further study. The suggestion to increase the number of seats for women was made by the members in the context of creating a more comfortable atmosphere for women to participate since they feel inhibited in a male-dominated body. Thus increasing the number of seats for women may help both in widening the range of representation as well as in improving the quality of participation.

However, having more seats for women is not an end in itself. Several members themselves questioned the advisability of increasing numbers without regard for selection of women according to their ability to participate. Furthermore, it is not a question of merely being selected from an elite class or a backward class that determines quality of participation of breadth of vision. Much depends on the value-system that is held by a society and the individuals who compose it. There are cases where it is noted that even among the backward classes or SC/ST groups, those who rise to privileged positions, develop an exclusiveness akin to that of the sophisticated upper classes, thus becoming alienated from their own people.

Increased representation for women on panchayat bodies must be accompanied by increased effort to create awareness of their role and responsibility as members. Women need to acquire greater self-confidence in order to make an effective contribution to the objective of panchayat bodies. It is more important to pay attention to the development of women at grass-root levels rather than create top heavy bodies in administration.

Participation at the village level

It was found that a small group of 25 respondents had high participation scores and many of these were found in the vicinity of big urban centres.

The rest of the 119 respondents live in villages and their social influence, when exercised, is manifested mainly in their own local surroundings This observation helps to focus attention on the need to develop leadership among women at grass-root level, namely, in the villages where women feel at home. They are familiar with neighbours, they do not have to travel far, they need not be away from home responsibilities for long. Thus social participation becomes easier. Though women are members at the block and district levels, it was evident that they found it difficult to travel around the block or district to get things done. They are acclaimed as leaders or organisers in their own villages.

A pressing reason for paying more attention to the development of local leadership is that established programmes like the CD/FCW/ANP have limited personnel who cover only a fraction of the villages in a block. In most villages there is no worker to initiate activities among women. Furthermore, the Evaluation Committee (Govt. of Maharashtra; 1971 : 237) has recommended that the posts of gram sevika and mukhya sevika be abolished and that gram sevikas be retained in the Samiti office, thus curtailing their work among women in the villages. It seems that there is a thinning out of such women personnel in rural areas, hence the greater need to rely on local women in the village population. Mahila Mandals are being encouraged but it is not merely the allotments of grants that can assure their effectiveness.

The gram panchayat offers possibilities for the training of women in social participation and leadership at the village level. It was encouraging to note the role already played by the gram panchayat in the present sample of respondents. Forty-two per cent of them had had the experience of membership at the gram panchayat level and six had even functioned as sarpanches. It is this group of women at the village level that should be the focus of training programmes.

Education of women-members

The important role of education in fostering greater social participation among respondents have been clearly highlighted in this study. The social, political and educational background of the family conditions the social outlook of women and helps to develop a sense of motivation to achieve more than what traditional culture ordains for women. Families that are socially active, usually see the advantage of education for their women and they encourage them both in the line of education as well as on the socio-political front. In this study, the reference to education usually means formal education of the type given in primary, middle or secondary schools.

While it is evident that education is necessary to increase social participation among women, a further question arises : What form of education can best serve the purpose—formal, non-formal? Much depends on the needs to be met and the goals to be realised. Much also depends upon the socio-economic background of each group. The elements in the educational system that have a bearing on the social participation of women need to be recognised with the possibility of application even outside the formal educational system for the benefit of older women who have not gone to school, and for those who cannot attend the regular hours of school.

This need for non-formal education is all the more important considering that the majority of women members belong to the older group aged over 40 years. It is equally important for those who do not dispose of much time outside working hours which have to be assured for daily subsistence. The study shows that even without many years of schooling, women show a fairly progressive outlook and a commendable effort to participate in local programmes. They manage to gradually overcome their timidity and embarrassment by living through the experience of membership. They have shown readiness to share their views on several social issues concerning marriage, the family, women's role, all of which show that the process of social awareness has already been stimulated by the wheels of social change around them. It is this potential that has to be recognised and which education should capitalise on. The study shows that the continuance of mere statutory representation of women or increasing their numbers on panchayat bodies will not result in any appreciable social change if women are not given the opportunity to be educated in the best sense of the word. Their innate talents seek creative expression, their capacity to know and understand must be filled, the desire to give of their best in collaboration with others, needs to be channelised in view of the common good. More programmes of education and training must be provided for those who are called upon to exercise a leadership role as and when elected or nominated on panchayat bodies. Educational opportunities should be made possible closer to the residence of village women. When women have grown to think, judge and act with confidence the present 'token' representation can give way to 'effective' representation which may obviate the need to depend on special reservation of seats.

Collaboration between women members of ZP/PS and women personnel in the Block

Women on panchayat bodies whether at the village, block or district level could be helped to work in collaboration with the mukhya sevika or gram sevikas appointed in the block. The expected role of the woman-member is that she be concerned with welfare or development activity for women and children in the block area. (Govt. of India; 1978 : 141). The mukhya sevika and gram sevikas are also trained to foster development by activities specifically meant for women and children. The goals for members and for personnel being the same, it is better to have co-operative functioning in the area. With such co-operation, activity undertaken in the block will obviously grow more effective. It was a matter of surprise to see at some of the interviews conducted by the researcher, when the mukhya sevika was present, that it was the first time she and the member had really met to converse. Yet, they have panchayat samiti meetings every month at which both are expected to be present. Perhaps social factors like 'caste' and 'class' between the panchayat member and the employed mukhya sevika account for the difficulty in drawing the curtain of communication.

During the course of her visits to various blocks and districts spread over the state, the researcher sensed that there was a kind of apathy to the question of women's development in several blocks, especially those situated in somewhat remote, interior areas of the states. The researcher also observed the mukhya sevikas and gram sevikas gradually lose their initial enthusiasm in the job due to lack of proper appreciation and guidance or follow-up of their activity. This has repercussions on the quality of work effected for women's development in the areas. If the quality of work at the grass-roots is poor, women remain unenthused and avoid participation thus slowing down the process of their own social development as well as the preparation to take responsibility at higher levels of the socio-political ladder. Yet those who know the field have to admit that in the villages only women can reach out to women, thus stimulating their desire for social growth.

In order, therefore, to ensure a certain continued focus on development activity for women, it may be desirable to create a special post for a woman at the level of a Deputy C.E.O. Her role would be to :

(1) effect co-operative functioning between women members and women personnel in the district. This is indicated in view of the thinning out of personnel employed as mukhya sevikas and gram sevikas as also because the vastness of rural areas makes it impossible to depend merely on employed personnel for the generation of development activity among women. One has to mobilise the present resources, both voluntary and public, more effectively. It is of the utmost importance that local women's leadership be developed if one wants to plan responsibly for women's increasing participation in the future ;
(2) co-ordinate the activities of various welfare agencies so that there may be a balanced out-reach to women in all parts of the district ;
(3) involve all classes of women in activity for development ;
(4) follow-up, guide and supervise the work undertaken by women-personnel employed under government auspices, in

the areas concerning development activity for women and children.

To respond to the demands of such a post, a trained social worker will be necessary. These suggestions are made to accelerate the process of social development among women in rural areas. This effort may not be necessary forever. However, at present women are a weaker section because they do labour under social handicaps and they are not in a position to compete on an equal basis with men, even though constitutional guarantees exist. They need certain special facilities before they can effectively give expression to the potential that lies within them.

The recognition of women's rights as a person and her social contribution during the national struggle for independence marked the beginning of women's social development in modern India. The years that followed independence have shown that the country has sought to give woman a status of equality with man in the constitution. The institution of panchayati raj has given expression to this democratic process but its positive impact for development will be experienced when people from every caste and class can find their place in the realisation of its objectives. Today women are needed who can stimulate the growth of leadership at the village grass-roots. The study has shown that women in rural areas are capable of progressive thinking and that they have the potential for valuable social participation. Many are the Ramabais, Anandibais, Savitribais who function even today in their rural surroundings.

The statutory representation provided for women on panchayat bodies is important not as end in itself but as a step forward in promoting women's participation in national life. It carries with it a hope—a hope that the present study justifies—to bring to the fore the rich contribution that village women are capable of making not only for the development of their rural sisters, but for the progress and peace of the nation.

BIBLIOGRAPHY

Abraham, Francis, *Dynamics of Leadership in Village India* ; Allahabad : Indian International Publications, 1974.

Altekar, A.S., *The Position of Women in Hindu Civilization* ; Delhi : Motilal Banarsidass, 1938.

Azad, R.N., "Integrated Rural Development" in *Dynamics of Development* ; ed. by S.K. Sharma, Vol. II; Delhi : Concept Publishing Company, 1977.

Baig, Tara Ali, *India's Women Power* ; New Delhi : S. Chand & Co. Pvt. Ltd., 1976.

Baig, Tara Ali, *Women of India*; Delhi : Publications Division, 1958.

Bass, Bernard M., "Some Observations About A General Leadership Theory" in *Leadership and Social Change* ; ed. by William R. Lassey ; Iowa : University Associates, 1973.

Bennis, Warren, "Post-Bureaucratic Leadership" in *Leadership and Social Change* ; ed. by William R. Lassey ; Iowa : University Associates, 1973.

Beteille, Andre, *Caste, Class, and Power : Changing Patterns of Stratification in a Tanjore Village*; Bombay : Oxford University Press, 1966.

Bhatt, Anil, "Dominant Caste and Political Process" in *Dimensions of Social Change in India* ; ed. by M.N. Srinivas *et al.* ; Bombay : Allied Publishers Pvt. Ltd., 1976.

Blalock, Hubert M. & Ann B. Blalock, *Methodology in Social Research*, London : MacGraw Hill, 1971.

Bombay, *Census of India* 1951, Vol. IV, Bombay, Saurashtra and Kutch ; Part I, Report and Subsidiary Tables, 1951.

Bope-gamage, A. & P.V. Veeraraghavan, *Status Images in Changing India* ; UNESCO Research Centre on Social and Economic Development in Southern Asia ; Delhi-Bombay : Manaktalas, 1697.

Brown, Mackenzie, "Traditional Concepts of Indian Leadership" in *Leadership and Political Institutions in India* ; ed. by Richard L. Park and Irene Tinker ; New Jersey : Princeton University Press, 1959.

Chandiramani, G.V., "Profiles of Women in Andhra Pradesh" in *Symbols of Power* ; ed. by Vina Mazumdar ; Bombay : Allied Publishers Pvt. Ltd, 1979.

Cheyney, Edward P., "Humanism" in *Encyclopaedia of the Social Sciences* ; Vol. VII-VIII ; New York : Macmillan Company, 1957.

Committee on the Status of Women in India, *Towards Equality* ; New Delhi : Dept. of Social Welfare, Govt. of India, 1974.

Cousins, Margaret, *Indian Womanhood Today* ; Allahabad : Kitabistan, 1941.

Dandekar, V.M. & N. Rath, *Poverty in India* ; Bombay : Indian School of Political Economy, 1971.

Desai, A.R., *Rural Sociology in India* ; Bombay : Popular Prakashan, 1969.

Desai, Neera, *Women in Modern India* ; Bombay : Vora & Co. Publishers Pvt. Ltd, 1977.

DeSouza, Alfred, *Women in Contemporary India* ; Delhi : Manohar, 1975.

Dubey, S.N. & R. Murdia, *Structure and Process of Decision-Making in Panchayati Raj Institutions* ; Bombay : Somaiya Publications Pvt. Ltd, 1976.

Edwards, Allen L., *Techniques of Attitude Scale Construction* ; Bombay : Vakils, Feffer & Simons Pvt. Ltd, 1969.

Emerson, Rupert, "Reflections on Leadership in the Third World" in *Modernization of Underdeveloped Societies* ; ed. by A.R. Desai (Vol. II) ; Bombay : Thacker & Co. Ltd, 1971.

Enthoven, R.E., *The Tribes and Castes of Bombay* ; Delhi : Cosmo Publications, 1976.

Everett, J.M., *Women and Social Change in India* ; New Delhi : Heritage Publishers, 1979.

Gajendragadkar, P.B., *Secularism and the Constitution of India* ; Bombay : University of Bombay, 1971.

Gangrade, K.D., *Emerging Patterns of Leadership : Comparative Study of Leadership and Social Structure* ; Delhi : Rachana Publications, 1974.

Ghildyal, U.C., "Behind Decentralized Democracy : Some Reflections on Administrative Behaviour" in *Behavioural Sciences and Community Development*, Vol. 4, Sept 1970, No. 2, 1970.

Ghurye, G.S., *Caste and Class in India* ; Bombay : Popular Book Depot, 1961.

Gibb, Cecil A., "Leadership" in *The Handbook of Social Psychology* ; ed. by Lindzey Gardner and Elliot Aronson, Vol. IV ; New Delhi : Amerind Publishing Co. Pvt. Ltd., 1975.

Gibb, Jack, "Dynamics of Leadership and Communication" in *Leadership and Social Change* ; ed. by William R. Lassey ; Iowa : University Associates, 1973.

Ginsberg, M., "Social Change" in *Reading in Social Evolution and Development* ; ed. by Eisenstadt : Oxford : Pergamon Press, 1970.

Goode, William J. & Paul K. Hatt, *Methods in Social Research* ; London : McGraw Hill Book Company, 1952.

Gore, M.S., "Traditional Patterns of Leadership in Rural India" in *Leadership and Authority* ; ed. by Gehan Wijeyewardene ; Singapore : UNESCO, 1968

Govt. of Maharashtra, *Report of the Evaluation Committee on Panchayati Raj* ; Bombay : Government Central Press, 1971.

Govt. of India, *Draft Outline : First Five Year Plan* ; New Delhi, 1951.

Govt. of India, *National Sample Survey* ; 16th Round, July 1960-June 1961, No. 159, 1970.

Govt. of India, *Recommendations of the National Commission of Labour* ; Delhi : Ministry of Labour, 1975.

Govt. of India, *Report of the Committee on Panchayati Raj Institutions* ; New Delhi : Dept. of Rural Development 1978.

Govt. of India, *Handbook of Social Welfare Statistics* ; New Delhi : Ministry of Social Welfare, 1981.

Hursh, Gerald Cesar & Prodipto Roy, *Third World Surveys* ; Delhi : Macmillan Company of India Ltd., 1976.

Inamdar, N.R., "Maharashtra" in *Patterns of Panchayati Raj* ; ed. by Ram G. Reddy ; Delhi ; Macmillan Company of India Ltd., 1977.

Inkles, Alex, "Making Men Modern : On the Causes and Consequences of Individual Change in Six Developing Countries" in *American Journal of Sociology*, Vol. 75, No. 2, 1969.

Jacob, George (Ed.), *Readings on Panchayati Raj* ; Hyderabad : National Institute of Community Development, 1967.

Jain, S.C., *Community Development and Panchayati Raj in India* ; Bombay : Allied Publishers, 1967.

Jain, S.P. & Krishnamurthy Reddy, *Role of Women in Rural Development*; Hyderabad : National Institute of Rural Development, 1979.

Jathar, R.V., *Evolution of Panchayati Raj in India*; Dharwar Institute of Economic Research, 1964.

Karve, Iravati, *Maharashtra : Land and People*; Maharashtra State Gazetteer General Series, 1968.

Katz, Daniel & Robert L. Khan, (Ed.), *The Social Psychology of Organisations*; New Delhi : Wiley Eastern Private Ltd., 1970.

Kaur, Amrit, "Women Under the New Constitution" in *Our Cause*; ed. by R.K. Nehru ; Allahabad : Kitabistan.

Keer, D., *Mahatma Jotirao Phooley*; Bombay : Popular Prakashan, 1974.

Kelkar, Govind S., "China's Women : The Change and the Challenge" in *Economic and Political Weekly*, Vol. XIV, Nos. 5 and 6, Feb. 1979.

Lakshmi Narayana, H.D., "Dominant Caste and Power Structure" in *Behavioural Sciences and Community Development*, Vol. 4, Sept. 1970, No. 2, 1970.

Lassey, William R., (Ed), *Leadership and Social Change*; Iowa : University Associates, 1973.

Lazarsfeld, Paul & Morris Rosenberg (Ed.), *The Language of Social Research*; Illinois : The Free Press, 1955.

Lerner, Daniel, *The Passing of Traditional Society*; London :The Free Press of Glencoe, 1958.

Levy, Marion, *Modernization and the Structure of Societies*; New Jersey: Princeton University Press, 1966.

Linton Freeman & others, "Locating Leaders in Local Communities : A Comparison of Some Alternative Approaches" in *Leadership and Social Change*; ed. by William R. Lassey ; Iowa : University Associates, 1973.

Maharashtra, *Census of India*, 1971 ; Series ii, Part II-A ; General Population Tables, 1971.

Mazumdar, Ammu & Menon, *Social Welfare in India*; Bombay : Asia Publishing House, 1964.

Mazumdar, V. (Ed.), *Role of Women in Rural Development*; Bombay : Allied Publishers Pvt. Ltd., 1978.

Mazumdar, V. (Ed.), *Symbols of Power*; Bombay : Allied Publishers Pvt. Ltd., 1979.

Mazumdar, V. & K. Sharma, "New Perceptions in Women's Studies" in *Economic & Political Weekly*, Vol. XIV, No. 3, Jan. 20, 1979.

Mehta, S.R., "*Emerging Pattern of Rural Leadership*" ; New Delhi : Wiley Eastern, 1972.

Mehta, Usha, "Indian Women and their Participation in Politics", in *Social Change* ; Vol. 8, No. 3, Sept. 1978.

Menon, L., "Women in India and Abroad" in *Women of India* ; ed. by T.A. Baig ; Delhi : Publications Division, 1957.

Mickelwait, Donald R., "*Women in Rural Development* ; Colorado : Westview Press, 1976.

Miller, D.C., *Handbook of Research Design and Social Measurement* ; New York : David McKay Company, Inc., 1968.

Muni, S.D., "Women in the Electoral Process" in *Symbols of Power* ; ed. by V. Mazumdar ; Bombay : Allied Publishers Pvt. Ltd., 1979.

Muthayya, B.C., "Leadership in Panchayats" in *Community Development and Panchayati Raj Digest*, Vol. 7, No. 4, April 1976.

Nachmias, David & Chava Nachmias, *Research Methods in the Social Sciences* ; London : Edward Arnold, 1976.

Narain, I. ; K.C. Pande, and others, *Panchayati Raj and Educational Administration* : Jaipur : Aalekh Publishers, 1976.

National Institute of Community Development, *Emerging Patterns of Rural Leadership in Southern Asia*; Hyderabad, 1965.

Nayar, P.K.P., *Leadership Bureaucracy and Planning in India* ; New Delhi : Associated Publishing House, 1969.

Nehru, R.K. (Ed.), *Our Cause*; Allahabad : Kitabistan.

Opler, Morris Edward, "Factors of Tradition and Change in a Local Election in Rural India" in *Leadership and Political Institutions in India* ; ed. by Richard Park and Irene Tinker ; New Jersey : Princeton University Press, 1959.

Pareek, Udai (Ed.), *Studies in Rural Leadership* ; Delhi : Behavioural Sciences Centre, 1966.

Pareek, Udai & T. Venkateswara, *Handbook of Psychological and Social Instruments*; Baroda : Samasthi, 1974.

Park, Richard & Irene Tinker, (Ed.), *Leadership and Political Institutions in India* ; New Jersey : Princeton University Press, 1959.

Patai, Raphael (Ed.), *Women in the Modern World* ; New York : The Free Press, 1967.

Phadnis, Urmila & Indira Malani, *Women of the World* ; Bombay : Vikas Publishing House Pvt. Ltd., 1978.

Punit, A.E., *Leadership Dimensions in Rural India* ; Dharwar : Karnatak University, 1973.

Rangnath, *Changing Pattern of Rural Leadership in Uttar Pradesh* ; New Delhi : Sindhu Publications, 1974.

Rao, V.K.R.V., "Thoughts on Social Change in India" in *Dimensions of Social Change in India*, ed. by M.N. Srinivas *et al.* ; Bombay : Allied Publishers, Pvt. Ltd., 1976.

Russell, R.V., *The Tribes and Castes of the Central Provinces of India*, Vol. IV ; Delhi : Cosmo Publications, 1975.

Sahay, B.N., *Dynamic of Leadership* ; New Delhi : Bookhive, 1969.

Scott, William A., "Attitude Measurement" in *The Handbook of Social Psychology*, Vol. II ; ed. by Lindey Gardner and E. Aronson, London : Addison-Wesley Publishing Company, 1968.

Sellitz, Claire and others, *Research Methods in Social Relations* ; Inc. Henry Holt & Co., 1960.

Sengupta, P., *Pandita Ramabai Saraswati* ; Bombay : Asia Publishing House, 1970.

Sethi, Raj Mohini, *Modernization of Working Women in Developing Societies* ; New Delhi : National Publishing House, 1976.

Shah, B.V., "Problems of Modernization of Education in India" in *Modernization of Underdeveloped Societies* ; ed. by A.R. Desai (Vol. II) ; Bombay : Thacker & Co. Ltd., 1971.

Shah, K.T. (Ed.), *Women's Role in Planned Economy* ; Report of the Sub-Committee on Women's Role in Planned Economy of National Planning Committee ; Bombay : Vora & Co. Publishers Ltd., 1945.

Singh, Avtar, *Leadership Patterns and Village Structure* ; Jullundur : Sterling Publishers Pvt. Ltd., 1973.

Singh, Andrea M., "The Study of Women in India. Some Problems of Methodology" in *Women in Contemporary India* ; ed. by Alfred Desouza ; Delhi : Manohar, 1975.

Singh, M.M., *The Constitution of India* : Calcutta : The World Press Private Ltd., 1975.

Singh, Y., *Modernization of Indian Tradition* ; Delhi : Thomson Press (India) Ltd., 1973.

Sirsikar, V.M., *The Rural Elite in a Developing Society* ; New Delhi : Orient Longmans Ltd., 1970.

Srinivas, M.N., *The Remembered Village* ; Delhi : Oxford University Press, 1976.

Srinivas, M.N., "The Social System of a Mysore Village" in *Village India* ; ed. by McKim Marriott : Chicago : The University of Chicago Press, 1955.

Srinivas, M.N., *The Changing Position of Indian Women* ; Delhi : Oxford University Press, 1978.

Tannenbaum, Robert and others, *Leadership and Organisation* ; New York : MacGraw Hill Book Co., 1961.

Tinker, Irene (Ed.), *Women and World Development* ; New York : Praeger Publications, 1975.

UNESCO, "Traditional and Modern Patterns of Rural Leadership and Authority in Countries of Southern Asia" in *Leadership and Authority*, ed. by Gehan Wijeyewardene ; Singapore : University of Malaya Press, 1968.

Vidyarthi, L.P. (Ed.), *Leadership in India* ; Bombay : Asia Publishing House, 1967.

Ward, Barbara, *Women in the New Asia* ; Paris : UNESCO, 1963.

Wilkinson, T.S. & P.L. Bhandarkar, *Methodology and Techniques of Social Research* ; Bombay : Himalaya Publishing House, 1977.

Index